TO MICHAEL, MY CONSTANT SUPPORTER, AND THE 'ANGELS' — INEZ AND JOSEPH — OUR MOST PRECIOUS CREATIONS! AND TO JOAN FRICKE, MY MOTHER, FOR TEACHING ME THAT TRUE STYLE STEMS FROM THE HEART, NOT THE POCKET.

ACKNOWLEDGMENTS

The creation of anything is never a singular venture. Whether it's an interior or a book about interiors, there are always many hands at work enabling a possibility to evolve into a reality.

And so it is with much gratitude that I thank … The visionary team at Murdoch Books, who dare to tread where others are too fearful. In particular Kay Scarlett for her foresight and for just 'getting it'; Diana Hill, for her gentle but persuasive approach to deadlines and for making me sound far less loquacious than I actually am; and Lauren Camilleri, for her innovative eye and her ability to keep her cool under extreme pressure! I take my hat off to you all!

My other family at The LifeStyle Channel, the original believers, for giving me a soapbox from which to spruik all things interior. And for allowing me to call 'work' what could be perceived by some cynics as 'shopping'!

Brigid Kennedy for sitting me down over a coffee and telling me to just get on with it — and how!

Photographer Prue Ruscoe, my friend and work comrade, whose beautiful, beautiful photographs give meaning to — and add much-needed relief from — my (many) words!

My personal support network — you all know who you are — without whom this book would never have been finished.

Of course, my deepest thanks go to the generous individuals for allowing us to photograph their homes, shops and restaurants as examples of what 'sense of style' and intuitive creativity are all about; and for their offerings of cups of coffee, tea and gourmet snacks during the process: Will Dangar; Helen and Mitchell English; Suzanne and Jim Mitchell (for their artworks also); Jill and John Ferrall; Lorna and Jason Marty; Liz and Brett Summerell; Carl and Alison Ryves; Julie Paterson and the team at Cloth; Scanlan & Theodore; and *my* dining paradise, Fratelli Paradiso.

sense of style

SHANNON FRICKE

colour

PHOTOGRAPHY BY PRUE RUSCOE

Hope you learn to mismatch to
imperfection! & Don't forget it's your
life that impact your surroundings;
make an imprint to preserve the
memories.

Love you millions

x x X

25-04-08
Rachel's 23rd

MURDOCH BOOKS

contents

page

the colour journey

I'VE ALWAYS HAD A FASCINATION WITH
THE WAY THAT PEOPLE LIVE, AND SO FOR ME THERE'S NOTHING MORE EXCITING
THAN BEING INVITED INTO A PERSON'S HOME.
I BELIEVE THAT SEEING HOW PEOPLE CHOOSE TO EXIST BEHIND THE DOORS OF THEIR
HOME IS THE ONLY WAY TO GET A REAL INSIGHT INTO
THEIR PERSONALITY, THEIR INTERESTS AND
THE TYPE OF LIFE THEY'VE CHOSEN FOR THEMSELVES.

As an interiors stylist and writer I've made a career out of being a professional sticky beak — and I get plenty of opportunity to walk through the front door of a diverse range of homes and to quiz the owners about their influences. All of the homes that I've been privy to see fascinate me in one way or another, and give me some insight into the people who live there. However, the homes that excite me the most, that make me feel as if I'm stepping into a world vastly different to my own, are the ones stamped with unabashed individuality. These homes don't subscribe to the whims of fashion, and they aren't always 'whiz bang' in their design. Instead, they're eclectic and personal; they reflect a lived and colourful life, and have their own sense of style. I can't necessarily imagine myself living in the same way — and that's exactly the point. These homes never fail to surprise and enlighten me, and I come away from the experience feeling like I know the owner that little bit better after being invited into their private world.

Given today's fast-paced lifestyle, it is difficult for most of us to find the time or the energy to truly individualize the way we live — to move against the tide with the aim of creating a path that suits the unique needs of ourselves and our family. The one place where I do feel I have some influence over my life is in my home. I believe that it's the aspect of your existence where you can, relatively easily, make changes to suit yourself. Your home is the environment that truly belongs to you, a place that you, and the people who share your life, have a real relationship with. When the outside world is moving too fast for you to bear, you can retreat to the personal world of home and derive strength and comfort from it. When you personalize your home you are being true to yourself: it's a form of honesty. To be content with your surroundings, and for them to nourish and serve you, you have to touch base with an honest sense of the way you want to live.

You hear the term 'sense of style' bandied around enough to think that we'd all have a grasp of its meaning, but in truth the idea is rather abstract and elusive. After all, if having a sense of style was that simple we'd all be bathing in its abundance! My interpretation of a sense of style is that it's simply a confidence; the casual ability to bring what seem to be disparate objects together in a room and make them look cohesive, as if they are just made to be united. In a way, it's the confidence to create an environment that is an extension of yourself. So, how do you go about developing your sense of style? Is it something that's exclusive only to the enviable few born with the knack? I don't believe so.

As I said above, I believe that style is something that evolves as a person becomes more confident about expressing the way they want to live and feel in their home. And the way to achieve this self-assurance when decorating your own home is to broaden your awareness and have your senses closely attuned to the world around you, to the environments you react to. Becoming more in tune with the way you feel most comfortable living is the first step towards unearthing a style that truly reflects your life.

It also helps if you understand the more practical elements that go into designing a room. Even though I've never been a great one for practicality, it is true that getting a grip on how a room functions creates an important foundation that will leave you freer to explore the creativity of decoration. By practicality I mean the principles of design such as scale, light, space, proportion, detail and of course the decorating 'glue' that holds it all together and which is the subject of this book — colour.

Colour is the aspect of style dearest to my heart, as it's the one with the most character — the cheekiest, if you like. It's the design element that makes a space come alive; it's full of energy, the life of the party. Colour is what stamps an interior with individuality, and it's one of the most useful tools to master when you're developing your own interior style. It's also the aspect of interior design that most of us really wrestle with: in fact, you could say that many of us have a love/hate relationship with colour.

It's understandable — after all, the choices are endless and constantly evolving, and the safety of neutrals seems like such a comfortable option when you are confronted by so many possibilities. But this is not a book about the comfort of familiarity. It's about unearthing style confidence and individuality, so I'm offering no place to get off the roller coaster ride that is decorating with colour. We're going to tackle its wonder head on, and in the process I hope to introduce you to a slightly different way of viewing the process of working with colour.

What you won't find here are the kinds of lecturing tools that you'd be used to seeing in other interiors books, for example colour wheels. Although I can see that they are useful for some people, I prefer to engage with instinct rather than be constrained by so-called rules and regulations. I don't believe that I could or should be providing you with some kind of prescription for using colour; how could I, when there are no rights or wrongs? Life and the way we live it is different for every person. Imagine having to live by somebody else's colour rules; you'd spend too much of your time trying to keep a grip on the dos and don'ts and not enough time simply seeing and experiencing for yourself — which is the only way to create a deeper understanding of the subject of colour.

For me, the relationship with colour and style evolves from life experiences and the effect they have on us. As a result, I have to warn you that instead of set-in-stone rules I've used a touch of good old personal nostalgia and a few stories to illustrate the effect that colour has on the way that I live.

Identifying a sense of style and a personal colour palette is a journey. As such it takes a certain amount of introspection and self-connection to confidently make choices about how you like to live in your space. Sometimes leafing back through your memories and unearthing patterns and choices that you are drawn to can help define how you like to live your life and what's important to you. It's a kind of 'self-help' approach; in this case, it's your interior that reaps the benefit! With this in mind, I've also approached the writing of *Sense of Style: Colour* as a kind of journey, with each chapter taking you to yet another level of colour awareness — hopefully ultimately leading to some sort of design enlightenment.

What you'll find here are suggestions for how to apply colour to illustrate your life and your home; how to break down the choices; how to use colour to help you develop a sense of style; and, most importantly, how to have some fun and a good-natured wrestle with this vast and crazy subject. I trust that anything you do glean from my view of colour and my experiences with it, merely sets you up for your own creative journey. I hope it will bring you one step closer to creating a home that reflects who you are; a home that mirrors the way you want to live; and best of all, a home that you love coming home to.

After all, isn't that what it's all about?

01
the
colour
of life

WHO ARE YOU? WHAT THINGS DO YOU LOVE?
WHAT MOVES YOU ? WHAT MAKES YOU SMILE? TO COLOUR YOUR INTERIOR IN A WAY
THAT REFLECTS YOU; FIRST YOU MUST
ESTABLISH WHAT MAKES YOU – YOU!

stop - don't move!

Don't think I've gone mad when I invite you, so soon into the book, to simply retire to some heavenly place and do . . . nothing.

Do bear with me; it may seem old-fashioned, but I believe that the simplest principles of living provide the best instruction. Life teaches us that to develop a relationship of any kind — whether with a person or even with food, or in this case with your personal colour palette — you must begin by simply being open to the possibility of it. I know this is tricky in a day and age when we allow ourselves such small increments of time for carrying out our daily tasks. But it is impossible to connect with anything if you don't give it exactly that — time.

Find a quiet part of the world — this could mean lounging in your living room, sitting in the park or lying on the beach — and just STOP. Live in the moment for a second, have a cup of tea to give yourself an excuse to just be still if you need to. You'll enjoy it, I promise. Then look at and absorb the wonderful colour combinations that exist around you. Engage your 'third eye' and simply think, see and feel; reconnect with your senses.

The modern world has taught us to neglect or ignore many of our most basic instincts. But without a connection to our sense of intuition it's almost impossible to gain any insight into how we react to our environment on an instinctive level — into what truly moves, excites or saddens us. So look around you. Think about what you're seeing: break it down into the smallest fragments of detail. How do colours connect with one another? What impact do they have on the way you feel? This is not a simple process. It would be easier to follow someone else's ideas — through, say, fashion — easier to settle for a quick fix, a bandaid measure; that way we wouldn't have to spend too much time in self-reflection. But I'm not convinced that following the conventions of colour and design is the way to live in peace with your space.

Understanding colour is to some degree a process of enlightenment. Remember that colour is not a mystery — it's always available to you, it's there every day, there are beautiful combinations in every corner of your world. Becoming aware of them is only the first step in your journey towards forming a relationship with colour.

AVOID DISHARMONY WHEN EXPERIMENTING WITH CLASHING COLOUR BY KEEPING THE BASE COLOURS IN YOUR ROOM TO A NEUTRAL PALETTE, AS HERE IN THE FLOORBOARDS AND WHITE WALLS (WITH JUST A HINT OF MAUVE ON THE MANTEL).

look around you

Now that you've settled, I'd like you to imagine, just for a minute, a world without colour: how boring a place would that be?

Everything viewed in black and white, with a shade of grey on occasion to break up the monotony — perhaps for some of you this may seem like an easier alternative; it certainly narrows the options and takes away a lot of the guesswork. But for a colour junkie such as myself this thought is almost too much to bear. You see, colour is my lifeline, the tool that I use most often to create my visual language; it provides me with endless hours of inspiration and discovery. Colour is an elusive and exciting subject that keeps me on my toes — just when I think I've got the hang of it, it will change. It's so seductive that I can't imagine how anyone could turn their back on it. I know at times dealing with it can be as tricky and tiresome as dealing with an overexcited child: it can come at you with all the force of a steam train and can be almost impossible to soothe down, leaving you tired, confused and exasperated. To establish a manageable relationship you must work in stages: stage one is just 'to see'.

NATURAL COLOUR

The world provides us with so many colour combinations and nuances, it's like looking at one very large colour chart. It's all there in nature for you to muse upon and interpret. Notice how the green of the trees hits the blue of the sky next time you're outside, or how the tones in the leaves of a eucalypt differ from those of a fig tree. Think about how the muted stone in a cliff face hits the blue of the sea, or the way electric blues and greens combine in a peacock's tail, or how the tones of lavender flowers in a field blend so perfectly.

Take the colour of an orange, for example. It will look different depending on whether you view it outdoors or indoors; in the same way its colour would change again if you were to look at it in a different country from your own, with different light. Think of the deep blue of the Mediterranean Sea compared with the aqua blue of the Caribbean, or the orange-red earth of Australia's Centre compared with the pink-red earth in Portugal.

ANYTHING — FROM THE PINK LIPS OF A CHILD TO ICE-CREAM FLAVOURS IN A CONE — CAN BE THE CATALYST FOR YOUR DREAM PALETTE. HERE, THE PLAYFULNESS OF PINK IS SUPPORTED BY A FOUNDATION OF LUSCIOUS CHOCOLATE.

1819

[SENSEOFSTYLECOLOUR] A CACOPHONY OF GREEN IS SAVED FROM LOOKING OVERWHELMINGLY MONOCHROMATIC THROUGH THE USE OF VARYING FORM, TEXTURE AND TONE.

'A JOURNEY OF A THOUSAND
MILES BEGINS WITH A SINGLE STEP.'

LAO-TZU

BEYOND NATURE

Nature is the starting point — how you are moved and how you react to different environments will give you some clues about the kinds of colours you could live with in your home. However, nature is not all there is when it comes to inspiration. Just as inspiring are the ways people have processed and reinterpreted the colours of nature and applied them to our built environment: the eccentric combinations of the tilework in a Gaudì building in Barcelona; the muted ochres of a villa perched on a hill in the Tuscan countryside; the bright red splash of a brand new Vespa motorcycle; the wild combinations in graffiti art. And let's not forget fashion, one of my favourite sources of inspiration; is there any more interactive example of colours in action than the clothing that we wear? Many a time the pairing of colours in a dress from my wardrobe has been the starting point for an interior colour palette. These are just some examples of the inspiration produced by creative people that you could use as a foundation when trying to work out how to infuse colour into an interior. As abstract as it may seem at first, the initial stage in developing a colour palette for your home is to see the colour around you, to interact with it and to interpret how those colours relate to each other. It's an intensely personal journey, and the trick is to take your time and just open your eyes.

[think beyond the obvious
[FASHION]

ON ITS OWN, BEIGE CAN COME ACROSS AS BLAND, BORING — BUT COMBINE IT WITH THE ELECTRICITY OF ANOTHER COLOUR, IN THIS CASE TONES OF BLUE, AND SUDDENLY A DYNAMIC PALETTE EMERGES.

Having to wear clothing is one of those unavoidable necessities of living: there is really little alternative. It's a social convention — we must dress to face each day. What's wonderful about clothing, though, is that creativity is born out of necessity, and talented designers are always looking for ways to spice up the monotony of it all. The result for us is that fashion is one of the most readily available and constantly evolving sources of inspiration that you can turn to, to ignite the creative juices. Every season designers reinvent their palette, and in doing so offer up a myriad of colours in all their different nuances for us to consider and digest.

I'm always looking to fashion as a guide for interior colour palettes, and I have a few favourites that have been the springboard for an interior or two. Missoni's unusual colour combinations appeal to my sensibilities: the way they cleverly combine strong neutrals with dramatic colour bursts is a perfect measure of balance. You would probably call the overall effect muted, which is exactly how I love my colours; just enough to keep you on your toes but not too much to overwhelm the senses. In Australia, Scanlan & Theodore have a similar approach, combining neutral tones with strong colour, but it's their more intricate patterning that I find most inspiring. And who could ignore the iconic fashion status of *Sex in the City*'s Carrie Bradshaw — this fictional character's whimsical approach to fashion reminds me that at the end of the day, creativity should be fun.

As always it's about doing your research to unearth what's new and exciting from the colour spectrum, and so at this point I recommend a day or two of window shopping to get a complete picture of what's out there. A good idea for those of you with a digital camera is to snap away at anything in the window display that inspires and moves you (generally, store owners won't allow you to take pictures inside their stores — they're worried about idea copyright!). Download the pictures onto your computer and start a file of favourites that you can draw upon when you need that creative spark. And of course, a small purchase along the way wouldn't hurt either — just for research purposes, you understand.

a colourful life

What does living a life full of colour have to do with developing a relationship with colour for your home?

For me, it's impossible to separate them. A life unpunctuated by colourful or defining experiences is as tedious a thought as living in a colourless world. I call it . . . living beige! The most evocative interiors that I have come across, the ones that display the individuality and sense of style that I've mentioned before, read almost like a book of the occupants' life experiences — all the way down to the colour palette.

If you think about it, every experience that you are exposed to can only add to your character in some way; in fact, your collective experiences ultimately form a storybook of who you are. They also give you clues about the way you feel most comfortable living and the types of colours that you feel happiest living with. It could be that you felt most at peace with yourself while sitting atop a mountain in Nepal taking in the muted tones of the landscape. Maybe the bright, clashing sounds and colours found in bustling Mumbai, India, truly brought you to life. Sometimes the simplest experiences can have the most resonance, like those that define your childhood. It's such a subjective thing; for example, your memories of summers spent with the family by the seaside could evoke a sensation of warmth and fuzziness, so much so that you want to immerse your home in bright blues and yellowy tones.

IT CAN BE A SINGLE ITEM THAT INSPIRES THE COLOUR PALETTE IN YOUR HOME. TURN TO THE COLOUR AND DETAIL OF YOUR OWN LIFE AND LOVES AS THE SPRINGBOARD FOR DEVELOPING AN INDIVIDUAL SPACE.

I'd like to think that the colour palette I've used to decorate my home is as diverse in scope as the experiences of my life so far. By way of example and at the risk of exposing just what a mishmash of colour I actually do live with, let me give you a taster — I'll start with the lounge room. With a colour palette of chocolate brown, burnt orange and bright green as its base, this room reflects a defining moment in my childhood, going back to when I was a mere toddler. You see, this was the orangey/brown colour palette that my mother used in our first home; a very old, but character-filled weatherboard cottage in inner-city Sydney. Sounds ghastly; and to be honest, for years I thought it was — even though it was very fashionable at the time (the early 70s). We only lived in this home until I was about five years old, but I have very strong memories of my time there, most importantly that I felt very happy and at peace, and so I guess there's just something nostalgic about the palette that left its imprint on my psyche. The bright green in my current home was creative licence on my part, and I'll let you in on that story a little later!

'COLOUR IS MY DAY-LONG OBSESSION, JOY AND TORMENT.' *CLAUDE MONET*

THE COLOUR OF MEMORIES

I've decorated the bedroom with a deep, steel blue and a European sand colour that is neither white nor yellow but a dirty kind of sand tone (I am loath to call it beige or even taupe), reflecting my love of spending time by the coast. The aqua highlights I've imported from a trip to the Caribbean. It doesn't matter which continent I'm on, it could be the coast of northern New South Wales or the east coast of Denmark, any time spent near or around the beach for me signifies that rare state of total relaxation and bliss which is almost impossible to get hold of these days. So it made sense to colour my bedroom, my place of sanctuary and rest, with this wonderfully meditative coastal palette.

I'm sure if you begin to reflect on your own life you will find some pattern of experience that has made its way into your home without you even realizing it. Reflecting on your life experience is a good place to start in developing your own sense of colour style. The best part about this process is that you can allow yourself to reminisce about all of the wonderful times you've had: go through old photographs of your travels — across continents or just through time — and see which of the memories that flood back give you a sense of satisfaction and joy. And if you look closely enough, I'm sure that you'll also notice a pattern of colour emerging.

feel

Let me begin by recounting a tale from a recent travel experience of mine. There is a purpose to it, and that is to offer you some insight into the profound influence that colour can have on how a person feels.

In this case sick to the stomach. Let me explain! I was lucky enough, not too long ago, to travel to Europe with some colleagues to film several television stories on designer hotels. After a long day of filming, the crew and I decided that the best idea for dinner would be to eat in our very swanky hotel's downstairs cafeteria. We'd heard the food was good, and as it was late and we had an early start the next day it seemed like the easiest choice. How quickly a good idea can turn sour! We made our way downstairs and as we eagerly pushed through the door, I was stopped dead in my tracks. I have to ask you to imagine the combination of colours that I saw before me. I'm talking bright, tomato red; acid-lime green; and a very shocking, electric blue . . . all thrown together in the same room and illuminated by the coldest, harshest arrangement of fluorescent lighting that I'd come across since my last visit to the dentist. 'I can live with this,' I thought, 'I'm starving after all!' So I chose my food and sat down with the others — none of whom (all men) had noticed the décor. All of a sudden, out of the blue, I was overcome by an intense wave of nausea. I started to feel light-headed and the room began to move, a sensation that quickly grew into downright sea-sickness. There was no question, I was going to throw up — and I hadn't even eaten yet. I had to get out of there. I had no choice. I left my dinner for the crew to finish and quickly made my way to higher ground before I was left humiliated. After scrambling back up the stairs, in search of a place where I could pull it all together, I found myself standing in the lobby amid a palette of cool pistachio green and chocolate. As quickly as it set in, the nausea abated and I was left feeling calm and settled. Needless to say, I ordered room service that night and I never ventured downstairs again.

COLOUR EFFECTS

There have been many books written on the psychological and physical effects of colour, its impact on your mood and your physical wellbeing — although none mention quite the reaction that I had! I'm not big on laying down rules about how things should make you feel — we're individuals after all, and just as lime green can excite one person, it can leave the next person feeling ill — but I do believe some universal truths apply to the effects of colour (which I go into in more detail in the next chapter). Having a clear understanding of the physical effect that colour has on you — whether it makes you calm, full of energy or even depressed — is another tool to help you make colour decisions for your home.

It's important to choose on the basis of commonsense and careful consideration. You may be a fan of red like me (berry not tomato in my case), but if you enjoy your sleep and/or are easily excitable, then it may not be the wisest option for you. I have always used a lot of red in my interiors; it's so intense and vibrant that I find it irresistible. However, I recently learned a very valuable lesson about being mindful of where I use it. My children, until a few months ago, shared a bedroom with a palette of aqua and red. My son, who's of a calmer, quieter nature, could cope with the excitement of the palette and had and still has no trouble sleeping amid it. My daughter, on the other hand, never slept well. My husband and I thought it was just her character (she's not one to want to miss out on any fun) until we decided to separate the two children and moved her across the hall. She now sleeps in a room decorated with pinks and mauves, still colourful, but not nearly as fiery — and guess what? To our surprise, she's been sleeping like a baby ever since. All that red was just too much for a girl who was born ever-alert and ready for a party. Needless to say, I wish that I'd written this book a little earlier in her life so that we needn't have endured so many nights of interrupted sleep; but as they say, what doesn't kill you makes you stronger. . .

'THE CHIEF ENEMY OF CREATIVITY
IS "GOOD" SENSE.' *PABLO PICASSO*

COLOUR INSPIRATION

DISPLAYING REMINDERS OF YOUR TRAVELS ON THE WALLS OF YOUR HOME REVEALS THE COLOUR AND TEXTURE OF YOUR LIFE.

[different lands
different colours
TRAVEL]

We are a generation of voracious travellers. Modern technology has afforded us the opportunity to move closer to each other and gain exposure to cultures rich in experiences vastly different from our own.

Every country has its own unique interpretation of colour influenced by its landscape, light and customs. Compare the bright, vibrant pinks found in an Indian sari to the warm and earthy pink of a Moroccan rug; the intricately patterned, golden tones of Balinese celebratory dress to the primary colours of African costumes. Even the bright colours of fresh produce found in the market in Thailand (red chillies, bright green limes) will vary from those found in the souks of Tunisia (saffron, cumin and cardamom).

I love the way the light diffuses colour in the northern hemisphere in countries such as Denmark, Norway and Sweden. The effect is luminous, almost whimsical, and the tones that the Scandinavians choose to colour-in their landscape, such as grey and pale blues, lend themselves perfectly to the play of the northern light. The density of the light and colours increases as you edge closer to the equator — the tones take on an intensity and a depth that are a direct reflection of their location.

But don't ignore the urban environments of the world's biggest cities either. Tokyo offers comic-book colour, for example through the Harajuku girls who parade every weekend in their baby-doll dress-ups as a modern-day manifestation of the geisha. In contrast, downtown Nolita in New York offers grungy tones of grey and black worn by the congregations of coffee drinkers who spill out onto the cobbled streets — the drab landscape punctuated only by the brightness of the yellow taxi cabs. Use your personal journeys and travel experiences to document your colour loves. When you travel, whether overseas or within your own country, try to be aware of the differences in colour and light, and use a camera to record the subtle variations. Remember, though, that the inspirational colours you find in different lands will change when you transplant them from their place of origin: colour is affected by the location and light in which it will be living; be mindful of this when applying what you've seen to your own home.

eat

Is it possible for taste – and I mean, quite literally, taste – to have an influence on the colour choices we make?

Could enjoying a bar of chocolate or devouring a roast leg of lamb subconsciously lead us down one particular colour path over another? (In this case it would be heart-warming brown.) It's true that we engage most of our senses when interacting with food; just looking at or smelling food cooking is enough to stimulate the appetite (or not, depending on what's on offer), but there's nothing like eating it to stir heartfelt emotion, whether it's fresh produce found at the markets or dinner cooked by your favourite chef. At its best the taste of food can leave you feeling satisfied, content and completely at ease with the world; at its worst, grouchy and downright bad-tempered! Just like colour.

It's worth tracking the constants in your food repertoire to see if you can find some thread of connection that will give you an insight into what kinds of colours move you. Of course, we all have the capacity to enjoy a wide range of cuisines — sushi lovers can be just as fond of a hearty stew — but if you try to separate intense yearning from merely eating for survival then you'll hit upon the thread that I'm talking about. I'm a hearty stew kind of girl myself: when presented with the choice I'll always head down the slow-cooked meat and veg path — the muted browns, oranges, greens and creams always stir emotion in me, hence brown and orange in my living room perhaps? In fact, brown is widely recognized as a colour of comfort, and of decadence as well as sustenance, when associated with food. A person's desire for chocolate in any of its varying forms is a great example of how food and the colour of food can have an impact on our emotions. This theory actually doesn't hold if blue is a favourite for you, as blue is one of the least appetizing colours in the spectrum — in fact, blue is widely recognized as an appetite suppressant, and as a consequence you won't find much in the way of blue food on the market.

The point of all this is simply to spark awareness that you should use all of the senses as tools when you are trying to build your personal colour profile. And of course, doing your research is the only way to get the true picture.

THINK OF COLOUR AS NOURISHMENT, JUST AS YOU WOULD THE FOOD YOU CONSUME. AT THE END OF THE DAY, IT SHOULD SIMPLY SERVE TO MAKE YOU 'FEEL GOOD'!

speak

Long gone are the days when we used single-word utterances to describe the colours around us.

Nowadays there is a name for every colour nuance. What was once simply blue has blossomed into aqua blue, sky blue, ocean blue, baby blue and so on. Brown is no longer just brown, it's chocolate, coffee, cappuccino, almond, camel, earth. The list is as endless as your imagination allows. And how you react to a particular colour — that is, the emotional response that you have to it — can be affected by the language used to describe it. If I were to preface the word 'brown' with 'chocolate', no doubt I'd evoke a warm, cosy and comfortable emotional response in most of you. 'Poo brown', on the other hand, definitely doesn't strike the same chord.

Culturally and politically, the language of colour is used to conjure emotion and evoke a particular feeling. For example, if you 'paint the town red' it means you are celebrating, kicking up your heels and enjoying life: red is the colour that signifies energy and excitement. If you say someone is 'green with envy'

then we automatically understand that this references an undesirable quality, a fault in a person's character: green is a colour associated with illness and imperfection. Being 'true blue' means that a person is considered to be reliable and faithful: blue is considered a steady colour, the sight of it lowers the heartbeat and creates a sense of certainty and calmness.

When it comes to our interiors we normally aspire to evoke positive emotion, and the importance of this is something of which paint companies are very aware. 'Honeycomb', 'Siena', 'Milk & Honey', 'Morning Light', 'Angel Shoes', 'Apple Crunch' (all from the Porter's Original Paints collection) are just some paint colour names that really appeal to my sensibilities. I couldn't think of anything more desirable than cocooning myself in honeycomb! And if painting my walls in 'Honeycomb' is as close as I'm going to get to it, then so be it. You should regard language as another tool available to you, along with your other sensory responses. Next time you find yourself describing a colour, think about exactly *how* you've described it, with fondness or disdain. Thinking about how certain colour descriptions move you — whether they are calming or exciting or nostalgic — will help you to inch one step closer to piecing together your true colour palette.

DOES YOUR INTERIOR SPEAK TO YOU HONESTLY? ONLY WHEN YOU LEAVE THE CAPRICE OF FASHION BEHIND CAN YOU CREATE A SPACE THAT TRULY REFLECTS YOUR PERSONALITY.

play

As with everything in life, when we are striving to master a skill, experimentation is the key.

You should not expect to be at the vanguard of decoration when you've barely dipped your toe in: it is not until you immerse yourself in the possibilities of any subject that you can truly master it. Naturally, the same goes for designing with colour. To compare your attempts with those of a die-hard professional who lives and breathes all things interior and colour is certain death for your self-esteem when you are at the outset of your journey. But take heart. The truly wonderful aspect of interior decoration is that if you don't get it right the first time, it is possible to rectify your errors. I know that economics plays a part in inhibiting the process of experimentation — it is fine for those with endless funds to dabble to their heart's content — but you won't ever successfully resolve your dream palette unless you make even a modest attempt.

Creating an interior is a process of evolution and discovery, and it will never be truly finished. As individuals, our character, likes and dislikes are constantly evolving and developing: the same goes for your home — it is a personification of you, after all.

The key is to move cautiously. Take your time. Enjoy the process of creating. Explore choices by taking the time to research. Photographs, pictures torn from magazines, snippets of fabric or ribbons, buttons, books, candle wax . . . whatever it may be, use the things around you, the things that speak to you, to build up a colour profile — and then dabble. Live with your collections of inspiration for a while before you move on a particular colour scheme. You may find that over time, the colour is not to your liking, and so the journey begins again.

Just as a child needs boundaries in order to truly flourish within this world of vast possibilities, so does your interior. Employing sound design principles (which I go into in Chapter 3) will help you create a framework to work within; you should always follow these principles to some degree. Without them, you could end up with a mishmash of a room — colour, pattern and form colliding with disastrous results.

Within these parameters, experimentation is what will get you to the place where you want to be — think of it as fun and you'll be halfway there.

USE THE COLOUR INSPIRATION FOUND IN EVERYDAY ITEMS TO YOUR ADVANTAGE. COLLECT ANYTHING FROM POSTCARDS TO BEADS TO INSPIRE YOUR DREAM PALETTE.

38**39**
[SENSE**OF**STYLE**COLOUR**]

[replace the colour wheel with colourful experiences ART]

Art is one of those joyous aspects of living that affect us on many levels — the subject, the form, the scale and of course the use of colour all work to arouse emotion and provoke thought. What kind of art do you love? Do you find the brightness and detailed form found in a Matisse or a Van Gogh uplifting? Perhaps the bizarre quality of a Picasso or Salvador Dali relates more to your sensibility.

For me it's the work of Mexican artist Frida Kahlo that stirs the strongest reaction. Kahlo was never shy about using bold colour in her work, nor was she afraid of living with it — which is very much part of the Mexican aesthetic. However, what I love most about her painting is the way she uses rather sombre tones over obvious brights. Frida Kahlo's appeal went beyond her paintings to the free-spirited life she led with husband Diego Rivera; a life she captured in the deeply moving, self-reflective portraits that have defined her as one of the most memorable artists of her

generation. Perhaps it's this desire to live with a kind of self-abandonment that I relate to most.

Spending time viewing art, whether simply for the form of it or for the meaning behind it, is a valuable colour resource: make a trip to an art gallery, or visit a bookstore to flick through publications on artists and their works. Colour is the tool that artists rely on the most in their work to help them illustrate and interpret their thoughts, so it's the best place to find a comprehensive approach to colour. For many artists, the colours they choose represent their state of mind; you can learn a lot about an artist's thought processes through their colour choices. Think of the luminescent colour combinations in a Matisse painting in comparison with darker, moodier tones found in many a Picasso. Think about how the colours chosen by each artist sit together and whether they work in harmony or against each other.

Become more aware of which art you are drawn to — not just the colour itself but the interpretation of the colour through the form. What better guide could there be for you when trying to discern your likes from your dislikes, as you work to define your personal colour palette. With this in mind, why not replace the tedium of the colour wheel with a Monet or Matisse for a true insight into colour in action?

ART ADDS AN EXTRA DIMENSION TO ANY SPACE. HERE THE OWNERS HAVE FEATURED WORKS BY LILY KARADADA (LARGE PAINTING TOP LEFT); NATALIE TUNGUTALUM (SMALL PAINTING BELOW LEFT); AND WILLY TJUNGURRAYI (PAINTING TOP RIGHT).

02
the
colour
palette

HOW DO YOU REACT TO COLOUR?

WHICH COLOURS AFFECT YOU JOYFULLY; WHICH NEGATIVELY?

UNDERSTANDING HOW COLOUR MAKES YOU FEEL

IS THE KEY TO HAPPILY COHABITING WITH IT.

colour moods

It's impossible to avoid colour. Colour is coming at us all the time, through both the natural and built environments, and it affects us in ways we are probably not even aware of.

If you think about it, colour is everywhere we look — on the street, inside our offices, on public transport, in shops, on television, on computer screens, in magazines, in schools, in cars, in bars; the list is endless. On top of that it has religious, political and cultural significance. Trying to make sense of colour can be overwhelming and downright confusing, particularly in this world so focused on technology and consumerism, where marketing hype is the cornerstone of our society and colours enter and leave our consciousness just as quickly as it takes a brand-new product to hit the shelves and be replaced by something more fashionable.

Have a think for a second about how many colours you would encounter during a shopping trip to the mall. Enough to blur your vision and too many for the human brain to cope with, I'm sure. It's no wonder most of us abandon the idea of using it in our homes; the place where we seek refuge from the world — the crazy world of clashing colour! It's not that we don't *want* to live with colour — after all, the joy that we derive from it is worth every cent — it's just that stopping our brain from spinning long enough to make the choices is a feat in itself. I hope that the first chapter of this book helped move you one step closer to coming to grips with colour, by recommending that you simply stop for a while. It's only when we do take the time to clear our heads by staring at a metaphorical blank wall that we can start to create some mental order. Once that mental order is achieved, the creativity begins.

Now that your awareness is sharpened you can start to measure your responses to colour and hopefully get a true, conscious indication of how it affects you as an individual. But what you may think is a simple process of defining your colour likes and dislikes is actually quite complex. As I briefly mentioned in Chapter 1, how colour affects humans on a physiological level has been the focus of much scientific research. Some colour therapists use it as a physical, emotional and spiritual healing treatment for their patients. Certain colours are known to increase the heart rate and blood pressure

COLOUR SHOULDN'T ONLY STIMULATE VISUALLY; IT SHOULD ALSO SERVE YOU ON A DEEPER LEVEL. HOW DOES IT MAKE YOU FEEL?

while other colours work in the reverse. Some scientists contend that every time we look at a colour, we experience, subconsciously or consciously, a physical response to it — hence perhaps the nausea triggered by the horror of my blue/green/red cafeteria encounter, described in the previous chapter. Research conducted in the USA into the effects of using particular colours in the interior of American jails found that prisoners living surrounded by a certain shade of pink displayed a marked reduction in aggressive behavioural patterns. Western colour traditions echo this finding; the bias towards pink being the colour of femininity, and its association with softness, gentleness, even weakness, still pervade our society today. Would you hesitate to paint your son's room pink, for fear he'd be perceived as too feminine?

How you react physically to a colour very much depends on your personality and mood. The feisty energy of red will affect a hyperactive personality in a different way than it would someone possessing a calmer nature. A normally laidback, relaxed person will have a different reaction to a colour when they are under stress or in a darker frame of mind.

The effect that colour has on a person depends not only on who you are and how you feel, but also on where you're at in life. Your relationship with colour is evolving; it's a moveable feast. What you relied upon as your colour palette in your twenties will be greatly altered by your forties, as your life changes and as you gain more experience of living. It makes sense to leave the fashion of colour behind, as it's impossible to keep up. The only way to feel truly at one with your home's interior is to identify a palette that fits the skin you're in.

COLLECTING COLOURS

As I mentioned earlier, I don't think that it's possible for me to offer you stock, standard mood responses to particular colours. However, I do think that each colour has some common element that every one of us can relate to. As you leaf through the following pages, think about how you're reacting to the particular colours you see there — and whether the colour moods that I outline relate to your experience. Look at how different colours sit together: how the blue of a wall works next to a red cushion, or a green chair next to a chocolate-coloured throw rug. Mull over the colours for a while; absorb them; live with them — make sure that your reactions are not merely a fleeting attraction. Create a mood board of the colours that you respond to most intensely. This could consist of almost anything: leaves from the garden; cotton thread; wool; fabric; bus tickets; magazine articles. My favourite device is photographs — generally ones that I've taken of my travels. If you start looking at your photos as a form of colour chart as well as a prompt to reminisce, they can give you a good indication of the colours that work for you.

[SENSEOFSTYLECOLOUR]

red Berry Tomato Scarlet Capsicum Henna Rose Cranberry Claret Garnet Ruby Cherry Saffron Wine

ALTHOUGH SHE IS HOT-BLOODED TO HER CORE, THIS RAG DOLL'S INTENSE REDNESS IS CALMED BY THE COMBINATION OF SOFT MAUVE AND PALE GREEN. WHO SAYS RED CAN'T BE TAMED?

'RED RINGS INWARDLY WITH A DETERMINED
AND POWERFUL INTENSITY.' *VASSILY KANDINSKY*

How would it be possible for red *not* to be the first colour in this section? The leader! Its very nature makes it impossible to ignore. Flamboyant, exciting and dynamic, red screams 'Look at me!' wherever it appears. It's alluring and sexy, but it can also be impetuous and difficult to pin down; its multifaceted nature leaves it open to so many interpretations. Red is simultaneously tempestuous and energy-absorbing, and life-giving and empowering — you have to engage fully with red to truly appreciate its wonder.

Red is the colour of fire — wild, hot and steamy; it's impulsive and difficult to contain, but at the same time mesmerizing and enchanting. It's the colour that we associate with danger — red traffic lights and stop signs are two of the most recognizable symbols of caution in our culture — but then for the Chinese it's a symbol of good fortune. Red also symbolizes stimulation, passion and sex. Red lips are after all considered the ultimate symbol of seduction. Cosmetic companies understand the power of red and are perpetually on a quest to find the perfect red lip colour — 'Carnal', 'Rage' and 'Lady Danger' are just a sample of the reds that you'll find in the MAC cosmetic range. For astrologers, red is the colour of the fire sign, Aries: courageous, determined and spontaneous — but also fearsome, obstinate and quick tempered. Red is the giver of life, being the colour of blood, the very thing that ensures our survival. For the ancient Romans, the red flag was a symbol for battle, where soldiers would spill blood to protect life. Snow White bit into a luscious red apple that led to her demise — a kiss on her sweet red lips, however, brought her back to life. It's the fine line that red treads, between danger and survival, that makes it the most alluring, arousing colour of the spectrum and one that is truly satisfying to decorate with — that's if you enjoy living on the edge a little!

The physical response that humans have to the colour red has been well documented because it's so obvious. Just a glimpse of red is enough to increase the heart rate and metabolism, leaving those who cast their eyes upon it in a subconscious state of arousal, their senses heightened and ready for action. Red is known to stimulate the appetite — notice whether or not you become hungrier when you're next dining in a red-decorated restaurant. And of course, consuming red food — think chilli and capsicum — can affect you so intensely that you are left in a sweat.

No doubt about it, it's an intense colour with a feisty nature, but that doesn't mean it can't be tamed to some degree. When choosing red for your home it's not so much a matter of whether you love it or you hate it; it's whether or not you can cope with living with it. Red's intensity can supersede all other aspects of a room if it's not given a boundary or two. The best way to manage red is to be mindful of how you react to it and where you use it. I mentioned in Chapter 1 my daughter's inability to sleep surrounded by a palette of red: she was already full of beans and filled with boundless energy, and sleeping in a red bedroom left her simultaneously wired, exhausted and out of energy. For the same reasons, red can provide a boost to those in need of some extra oomph.

With this in mind, it's important to track how you react to red before you employ it in your home. Are you an overzealous type with boundless energy, prone to hyperactivity? Or are you more laidback, prone to lazing around, kicking back and taking life as it comes? As well as yourself, think about the dynamic of your family before you embark on the red journey — how you engage with each other within the context of your home. Which areas of your home could cope with a little extra 'bite'? Think about your life and what you need to get from it. Are you currently in a bit of a rut, unable to gain momentum and energy for life? Then perhaps red will give you the stimulation that you need. Is your life already dynamic, stressful and in need of taming? Then avoid red unless you love the unpredictable thrill of it all.

[SENSEOFSTYLECOLOUR] YELLOW AND EVEN PINK ARE ALSO GREAT COMPANY FOR RED.

RED AND BLUE MAKE FOR A DYNAMIC PARTNERSHIP. HOWEVER, GREEN, BLACK,

What kinds of activities take place in what parts of the home? Which areas are the site of action; which areas require calm? Need to spice up your sex life? Touches of red in the bedroom could move you closer to passion: think cushions, trims, a red-patterned rug perhaps. Too much red, however, could leave you feeling overwhelmed and unable to rest properly, so maybe you should leave the red walls for the playroom instead. The playroom is a wonderful place to experiment with red; it is after all designed to promote stimulation and interaction — just look at the amount of red toys on the market. And you shouldn't forget the kitchen, where even a few accents of red will leave the family salivating at the thought of your cooking.

Not all reds are created equal, and the various tones all work to create different responses in different people. Just the thought of bright, tomato red leaves me feeling sick to the stomach in the same way that tomatoes do. Cherry red on the other hand brings me sheer joy, so much so that eating ripe cherries in the summertime is one of my favourite indulgences. Raspberry red . . . so so! Burgundy . . . too sophisticated, too grown up! How you react to red is an entirely personal response. Don't let its power and its confrontational nature put you off. The trick is to move cautiously — start by painting one wall red and see how you like it before you move ahead with the others. Live with a red cushion or throw rug for a while to see whether or not you can really stand its presence. Start with a pattern where red is the understudy rather than the star. You'll know the effect that it's having on you immediately — and if you like it, keep adding more. Before you know it, you and red might have become good friends. And if you do, then you can be certain that you'll be friends forever!

RED WORKS WITH ...

Other warm colours, such as orange and yellow in their various tones. Deep muted shades of plum give it some grounding while the more fresh and youthful shades of blue such as aqua give it an extra kick. Neutrals, such as oatmeal or chocolate, when teamed with red help to tame its feisty nature.

RED WORKS WHERE ...

Keep red to action rooms such as the kitchen, dining room and playroom. Avoid bedrooms, unless your life could benefit from a little extra action!

RED CAN SUPERSEDE ALL OTHER ASPECTS OF A ROOM — IT NEEDS BOUNDARIES.

green Apple Lime
Olive Grass Moss Gum
Pistachio Jade Avocado Melon
Mint Teal Khaki

GREEN HAS THE POWER TO IMPASSION — ONE PIECE JUST ISN'T ENOUGH. PERHAPS IT'S BECAUSE GREEN CONNECTS US WITH NATURE, WITH THE TREES AND PLANTS AROUND US, WITH THE VERY THINGS THAT ENABLE LIFE TO THRIVE.

I'm having a love affair — with green! Sounds crazy I know, but if you've ever been in love with a colour then you'll understand how it feels. Your heart races, your stomach knots and you break out into a gentle perspire at the merest glimpse of it. I wasn't expecting to fall so deeply in love with green; I'd dabbled with green before, but it had let me down (which goes to show that choosing colours can sometimes be all about the timing).

Green and I met around the time that my husband and I bought our first home. Eager to mark our arrival and make the home ours, we decided that some changes were in order. The exterior desperately needed a facelift, and transforming it from its existing shade of dark, sombre blue to a more uplifting colour seemed like the obvious place to start. I wanted to find a colour that would be 'our' colour, which reflected our individuality and our beachside location. There was a lot riding on my choice: my reputation as a creative risk-taker for one, but on top of that the reality that I would have to look at my decision for many years to come.

I always look for inspiration in less-obvious places: great ideas can be hiding in anything from a certain shade of bubblegum to bird feathers. So with the pursuit of individuality in mind, I turned to my first port of call, my library of magazines. At the time I was consumed by all things southern French (it was the mid 90s), so naturally I began by flicking through pages filled with this aesthetic. I loved the way the warm, dusty, almost hazy French landscape was punctuated by the piercing blues and greens used in the details of the stone-clad houses.

Before you could say 'vive la France' I had found a colour to fit the bill. Imagine this if you can: a magazine photograph of a home built on the warm, dusty French earth featuring a rustic, French . . . swimming pool. It wasn't just any swimming pool — this pool was filled with the most inviting milky green water, the surface gently ruffled by the warm French breeze. I'd never seen a green quite like this one before — it was muted, almost chalky. This was the colour that would coat my new home.

Undeterred by the fact that my colour of choice was like that of milky green water, I headed straight to the paint shop, photograph in hand, to try to secure a perfect match. That it only took a few attempts at mixing simply reinforced my confidence: I bought the paint, booked the painter and waited for my home to be transformed.

The big day arrived and with confidence to spare I headed off to work, leaving the painter to weave his

magic. Unable to contain my excitement for the duration of a whole day, I decided to head home early, to see my new house in all its daylight glory.

But as my home came into view, I was struck by the most excruciating sense of disappointment. There it was, my green house, staring accusingly down at me, a freak from sideshow alley. I'd made a huge mistake — green and I had not worked out. Deeply embarrassed by my blunder, I did what anyone would have done in my situation — I ran inside, locked the door and kept the lights off hoping none of my friends would drop in for a visit. The next day, I left for work in the dark, called the painter and suggested that perhaps the safety of white would be a more appropriate tone for my beloved home. Like all good tradespeople with their futures in mind, he agreed. And with that, it's been white ever since.

As you can imagine, I was unable to look green in the face for a long time — it had been so cruel to me. Green and I were off, and I had to face the reality that our relationship had been merely a one-night stand. Then about two years ago I came across it again, by chance. It wasn't the watery, immature green that I'd encountered before. This time it was an upfront, bold green — a green with confidence and depth. I couldn't resist. I moved cautiously at first, a painting here, a cushion there, not wanting to make the same mistake twice. But before long, green was making its way back into my heart. I spray-painted a chair, added a throw and an ornament or two. It took some time, but now green and I are completely in love again. And because I've come to this relationship with a balance of both head and heart, I have faith that this time around, green and I will be together forever!

I'm fully aware of how mad my love for a colour might seem, but it does raise the question: out of all the colours in the spectrum, why have such a deep, emotional response to green? Perhaps it's because green has the highest number of nuances visible to the human eye; that is, our eye can recognize more shades of the colour green than it can of any other colour. Just think about the vast array of greens that exist in our natural environment: from bright green grass to a luminous turquoise lake or deep green, slimy moss and everything in between.

There are so many greens in the world and most have a connection to nature — our natural environment is predominantly green. Green plants help provide us with the oxygen we need for survival; could it be that green is quite literally a breath of fresh air? During those times in your life when you feel a need to reconnect with the earth, with nature, is it possible that coating your home in green could aid the process?

The fact that green is smack bang in the centre of the colour spectrum, the great balancer, adds weight to the idea. Green evokes harmony and relaxation and is the colour of choice for those wanting this experience in their homes. If you've ever visited a health spa, you'll know

SAVE BRIGHT GREENS FOR THE ACCENTS IN YOUR DECOR. IF YOU WANT MORE, THEN STICK WITH CONTEMPORARY, MUTED SHADES.

'GREEN, I LOVE GREEN.
GREEN WIND. GREEN BRANCHES.'

FEDERICO GARCIA LORCA

that green is often the preferred decorating colour as it's the generator of calm. In the world of show business the 'green room' is the place where entertainers sit to relax and connect before a performance. So, in this sense, green equals tranquillity, peace and new life.

But it very much depends on the shade! While for some people green represents harmony, for others it's a predatory symbol. Think about how many green monsters you've encountered in science fiction films. We often associate illness and decay with the colour green; and 'envy', one of the seven deadly sins, is also signified by green. Choosing green as a decorating tool for your home comes with a warning — be sure of your choices.

Pure, bright greens will uplift you, conveying energy and life. Murky, khaki greens will envelop a space and close it in. Again, the trick here is experimentation. The wonderful thing about green is that the right shade can be used extensively, to add life to an interior. I've seen rooms that are almost completely green, of varying tones that all work harmoniously together. Other spaces, generally those lacking light, can cope with only a smattering. Deep, murky greens like khakis and olives should be kept for the accents only. Gentle sage greens make a perfect backdrop on walls. Racing green conveys a sense of sophistication and heritage. Green is such a tangible colour, and it pairs beautifully with many other colours, such as purple, chocolate, blues, pinks and the deeper tones of red, which makes it a good place to start on your decorating journey. My advice is to keep it measured for starters, as the right balance of head and heart will protect you from ending up in a pickle. Trust me, I know.

GREEN WORKS WITH ...

Other shades of green for a dose of relaxation. Pair with blue for a feeling of cleansing and calm. Chocolate and deep rich creams will provide your green with a dose of sophistication.

GREEN WORKS WHERE ...

In areas of the home needing calm and serenity such as bedrooms; and in bathrooms and lounge rooms, which are primarily used for relaxation.

purple Mauve
Plum Lilac Hydrangea
Periwinkle Iris Grape Indigo
Jacaranda Lavender Aubergine

[SENSEOFSTYLECOLOUR]

PURPLE IS SUCH A COMMANDING COLOUR — SOMETIMES A MERE GESTURE IS ALL THAT A ROOM NEEDS. HERE, A BUNCH OF LILAC FLOWERS ADDS A CERTAIN PRESENCE TO THIS AUSTERE BLUE PORCELAIN SINK.

Have you ever seen an expanse of purple flowers growing in a field? If so, then, I'm sure that you remember exactly where you were at the time. No doubt you were meandering through the depths of the countryside. It was probably spring time — the weather was warm, but not hot, and there was a gentle breeze blowing as you took in the breathtaking landscape of purple spread out before you. There's something innately commanding about the colour purple, especially when viewed in nature. Perhaps it's that, in comparison with the other colours in the spectrum, purple is so rarely seen; we are very seldom graced with its presence. If you think about it for a second, how often do you come across it growing wild? We see plenty of blue, green, yellow and pink in nature — but purple? Its scarcity makes it alluring, special. We are allowed merely an enticing smattering which keeps us begging for more.

'I THINK IT PISSES GOD OFF IF YOU WALK PAST THE COLOR

PURPLE IN A FIELD SOMEWHERE AND DON'T NOTICE IT.' *ALICE WALKER*, THE COLOR PURPLE

Our earliest ancestors treated the colour purple with the same reverence as they did nature itself. From ancient times the use of purple was reserved for those of high rank, worn by emperors and kings — thus the expression, 'to be born in the purple'. Historically, purple dye was the most difficult to source: extracted from the glands of the murex shellfish (originally by the ancient Phoenicians), it was available only to the wealthy and privileged. Mystics, wizards and clairvoyants, those possessing a high degree of intuition or special powers, are often represented wearing the colour purple — even the great Dumbledore from the Harry Potter books wears a purple cloak on occasion. No other colour from the spectrum symbolizes fearlessness, strength and a devotion to duty quite like purple does.

Created using a mix of red and blue, purple is the balance between hot and cool. It simultaneously evokes strength and subtlety, the blue taming the feistiness of red and the red adding character to the tranquillity of blue. Adding more red will enliven purple; blue will calm it down. Purple in all its tones, from mauve through to indigo and aubergine, works to encourage contemplation and thought. Those who dabble in colour therapy believe that the use of purple in your life can lead to a higher sense of self-awareness and spirituality; people with an indigo aura possess divine knowledge and a higher mind. It makes sense, then, that if what you need is a dose of enlightenment in your life, purple in all its variations is the colour for you. But if too much introspection is getting you down, keep well away from this powerful colour; you might end up trapped in a spiral of self-reflective tail chasing.

THERE ARE SO MANY TONES OF PURPLE TO CHOOSE FROM. EACH WITH THEIR OWN CHARACTER. ALMOST ANY COLOUR CAN BE PAIRED WITH IT — JUST ENSURE YOU MATCH THE UNDERLYING QUALITY OF EACH COLOUR. THAT IS, BRIGHTS WITH BRIGHTS, PASTELS WITH PASTELS, AND MUTED TONES TOGETHER.

How, then, does purple relate to a contemporary aesthetic? The trick to using it in a décor is to think about it tonally and to be sure of where it works best in the space. You probably wouldn't use the intensity of pure purple to coat your walls, but soft lavender is an interesting alternative to white, adding an element of colour without being overwhelming. Deeper tones are ideal for accents: pair bright purple with other complementary colours such as blue, green and pink in your upholstery, or use it for a feature wall if you're only after a taster. If soft, pastel tones are too feminine for your environment, play with the more intense shades of grape and aubergine for a distinguished twist. Look carefully at your space and its aspect before choosing a tone. Rooms bathed in natural light work well with the brighter, bluer shades of purple such as indigo and jacaranda, uplifting the space and giving it energy. Darker rooms, which lend themselves to an air of sophistication, benefit from the more complex shades of grape and plum.

You may think that these deep tones will make your room seem darker, which can be the case, but with purple it's a good idea to go *with* the room rather than against it. A prissy mauve will leave your room not only dark, but also cold. The deeper shades that contain more red are the way to go here. Kitchens tend to be an ideal place to employ purple — not just on the walls or window treatments, but also through accessories such as dinnerware and glassware. Bathrooms work in the same way. And of course, it's perfect for children's bedrooms, particularly if you want to tread the fine line between the space being suitable for either a boy or a girl.

The most important thing is to keep your shade of purple current. When embarking down the purple road you do run the risk of your interior looking overly pompous or even worse, twee; to avoid this, ensure that you pair your purple with streamlined shapes in your furniture and a more modern aesthetic overall. Upholstery is always a safe bet, as are cushions, throw rugs and the like where purple works as a highlight only. Sometimes, a few purple flowers in a vase is enough. Take the lead from mother nature and keep it as a specialty colour rather than the focus. This will ensure that your interior stays relevant and relaxed.

PURPLE WORKS WITH …

Muted shades of purple such as plum and aubergine combine beautifully with soft, muffled tones of green. Pure purples combine with upbeat shades of blue such as cobalt, or you can keep it tonal by using lighter and darker shades of purple.

PURPLE WORKS WHERE …

Bedrooms appear immediately more opulent when decked out in purple. Soft shades represent an alternative to pink and blue in little girls' and boys' rooms.

orange Peach
Amber **Poppy** Sienna
Pumpkin Terracotta Mandarin
Mango Apricot Tangerine

ORANGE IS SUCH A FUN COLOUR — HOWEVER, IT DOESN'T HAVE TO BE OVERBEARING. YOU CAN TURN THE INTENSITY UP OR DOWN: BRIGHT ORANGES WILL DRAW YOUR FOCUS, WHEREAS A MORE EARTHY ORANGE — TERRACOTTA, FOR INSTANCE — WORKS HARMONIOUSLY WITH THE OTHER ELEMENTS IN A ROOM.

Why is it that orange has fallen from grace in the world of interior design over the past few years? It's such a fun colour, after all! In fact, not since the 70s, an era that embraced social freedom and the pursuit of a good time, has orange stepped onto the centre of the decorating stage. Could it be that over the past few decades we have been taking our interiors all too seriously; so much so that we haven't been able to see past a currency of black, white, grey and neutrals? It's hard to believe that orange, with its sunny disposition and beaming quality, could be so very pointedly overlooked; or, moreover, blatantly ignored! Is it that orange is simply just too happy to be taken seriously; too frivolous to be seen as cutting edge?

It's not that orange has been dropped entirely — you'll often see it beaming out from supermarket shelves as the preferred colour for everything from your favourite soft drink to suntan cream; the fact that it's often used to attract a quick sale has meant that it has also been tainted as too disposable (read: cheap) to use in your home décor, a place where your choices are expected to endure the test of time. But don't overlook its attributes — it has so much to offer if you just open your heart to it. Orange is the colour that induces in us a feeling of warmth, sensuality, fun and most of all creativity, its sunny-ness eliciting a positive reaction in any person who gazes upon it. Colour therapists say that those who surround themselves with orange feel cocooned and protected by the warmth of the shade, which in turn gives them the confidence to initiate new projects — just what you need if you're suffering from a bout of procrastination. Its detractors claim that it's a childish and flippant colour — but in my opinion the world could do with a little more of these two characteristics anyway. As orange has become the colour representing resistance movements around the world, signifying strength and bravery, I think it's only right that we fight to keep it alive in the world of interiors! Long live orange, I say!

A lively mix of red and yellow, orange possesses the energy of red but without the rowdiness; and the happiness of yellow without the persistent optimism. It encompasses everything from bright, acid shades through to earthy, dusty tones; not forgetting the soft peach and salmon hues that were preferred, generally paired with grey, in the early 80s. The warm shades of ochre, with their reference to the Tuscan earth, have been popular in recent years, particularly as an exterior paint colour. A deeper, earthier shade of orange, ochre relays a seriousness and a sense of sophistication that you just don't find with the sunnier shades. Perhaps this accounts for its popularity, or perhaps it's just as close as we'll get to having a little piece of Tuscany for ourselves. Maybe it's just that ochre as the colour of the earth simply connects us with the land, grounding us. If you've ever walked across the orange sand of a desert, you'll appreciate how much of a spiritual experience that can be. With this in mind, one idea is to add orange as a floor covering when looking for ways to infuse it into an interior — it provides wonderful grounding for a room. A rug is probably the most contemporary use; wall-to-wall carpeting may be too much! Although I have used orange paint to coat walls in the past, most experts would disagree with that practice, saying it would be too overpowering; too energizing to live with on such a grand scale. Even though it does take a few coats to overcome porosity, it is definitely worth it if you're up to living with the enthusiasm of orange. The bathroom is a great place to experiment with this uplifting colour as well, as it's just the room where you can afford to instil a sense of energy and stimulation. And a collection of orange mosaic tiles lining the walls is sure to achieve that. Touches of orange in the kitchen, again through tilework or as a highlight colour in the accessories, is guaranteed to keep your enthusiasm for food preparation alive. Overall though, I'd keep the brighter shades to a minimum. You do run the risk of your space becoming overly psychedelic, which is the mistake that our 70s forefathers made — leaving us in a state of orange overkill for decades. As they say, too much of a good thing. . .

'ORANGE IS THE HAPPIEST COLOUR.'

FRANK SINATRA

Where does this leave the peachy, salmon and apricot shades of orange then? Although out of vogue in the recent past, even more so than the vibrant shades if that's possible, these softer tones of orange do still have a place in home décor. Keep them up to date by ensuring that the shade you choose, although it can be soft, is not too insipid, thereby negating its very presence. Substantial, weighty shades of peach/salmon/apricot work well in a mix. Keep it bite-sized by using it as part of a pattern or as the base colour for an armchair. My advice is to never, ever attempt to coat the walls in this colour — its overuse in dental surgeries in the 80s has assured its place in decorating hell!

All in all, the trick with orange is to have fun with it. If living with it inside the house is too much to begin with, try it as an accessory outdoors. Contemporary plastic outdoor chairs — along the lines of Marc Newson shapes and designs — work well in this lively shade. Keep the shapes simple and the patterns geometric (think Marimekko), and you're sure to do this exciting colour the justice it deserves.

ORANGE WORKS WITH ...

Reds and yellows in spicy shades. Burnt orange is perfect with chocolate brown and shades of amber. 'Notice me' shades of green add some punch to an orange palette.

ORANGE WORKS WHERE ...

Anywhere that could do with some energy and humour, such as lounge rooms, kitchens and even bathrooms.

ORANGE INDUCES A FEELING OF WARMTH, SENSUALITY, FUN — AND CREATIVITY.

[SENSEOFSTYLECOLOUR]

yellow Lemon
Mustard Gold Sunflower
Canary Banana Maize Daffodil
Buttercup Custard Saffron

RICH TONES OF MUSTARD CARRY ALL THE POSITIVE ATTRIBUTES OF YELLOW BUT HAVE AN AIR OF SOPHISTICATION. PAIR WITH BLACK, CHOCOLATE AND CREAM AND YOU HAVE A LUXURIOUS AESTHETIC, IDEAL FOR A LOUNGE OR BEDROOM.

'. . . EXPERIENCE TEACHES US THAT YELLOW
MAKES A THOROUGHLY WARM AND COMFORTING IMPRESSION.'

JOHANN WOLFGANG VON GOETHE

It's undeniable that of all the colours in the spectrum, yellow is the most optimistic. In fact, it has to be said: yellow is relentlessly cheery! So much so that this colour — permanently 'switched on' and ready for action — could be accused of bordering on the annoying. There is no time to relax when yellow is around, and if you're the type who likes their interior to be laidback and lazy, don't dwell too much around this end of the colour spectrum. But those in need of a little extra happiness in their life or a boost in confidence could benefit greatly by getting down and dirty with this life-of-the-party shade.

One of the three primary colours (red and blue are the other two), yellow is probably the most eye-catching colour of all. Your eye can't help but be drawn to it, particularly the brighter shades; its luminosity ensures your attention. Because of this, yellow is a colour that you'll see a lot of as you move through your day. It's associated with road safety in most countries and is used in everything from road signs to local authority trucks to make you aware of every possible danger. Children wear yellow raincoats so they will be seen by drivers in bad weather. In Australia, it's the colour, coupled with red, of a lifesaver's uniform and of a life jacket. It's worn by firefighters in action. And who could forget the yellow taxi cab, a symbol of fun-loving and optimistic New York City? Those who work in the arena of graphic design understand its power and allure and as such it is used as a marketing tool, drawing your attention to everything from banners to magazines. Next time you're at the newsstand, see whether or not you're attracted to the magazines with yellow type over the others — you'll be surprised at the subconscious effect.

Because of its sunny disposition, yellow is often associated with celebration (Hindus wear it as part of their celebratory dress) and symbolizes hope. In imperial China it was worn only by the emperor, and in South-east Asia it's still regarded as a royal colour. In China it's considered the colour of intuition and wisdom, and legend has it that it was preferred by the wisest of characters, Confucius himself. Gold, one of the most precious metals, is of course a token of good fortune. There seems to be no denying it; wherever there's yellow, there's good fun to be had by all . . . or is there?

Sadly, the truth is that it's not all fun and games when yellow is about, and it very much depends on your personal associations as to whether or not you can see yourself living with it. Just as it can be seen as a sign of happiness, it can also be seen as a sign of illness and moral weakness. Such is the duality of colour. Jaundice, the symptom of a malfunctioning liver, turns the sufferer's skin an insipid shade of yellow; in general, people who are unwell have a yellow cast to their complexion. A person who is considered to be a coward has a 'yellow streak', a reference to their weakness. In medieval France, the doors of traitors were painted yellow.

But if you decide to put all of that aside and head down the 'yellow brick road', then what's the best way to go? As always with colour, it's important to keep it relevant to you and to the decade that you're living in to prevent it looking like an impostor from another era. Traditionally, we tend to associate yellow in all of its incarnations with the gaiety of chintz and flowers, the kind that you would find in old-world interiors; but that's not the only way that you can infuse it into your home. If you are interested in the brighter tones, then strong, clean-lined geometric patterns lend themselves beautifully to yellow — the boldness of the shapes works well in toning down the giddiness and movement that the eye associates with this colour. A brighter yellow works best as an accent in a room; making it the star could leave you feeling a touch sea-sick. Paired with grey, yellow makes for a very contemporary environment.

LIVING HOME

LOVE

LO STILE
ELLE DECOR

...All you need is love. Musica profetica quella dei Beatles. L'abbiamo scelta come colonna sonora virtuale del nostro numero di Natale. Interni ricchi di calore, idee di tradizione, idee regalo e di decorazione... senza retorica, con affetto. Auguri da tutti noi

ABORIGINAL ART, SCULPTURES FROM ASIA
AND RICH, ETHNIC TEXTILES COMBINE TO
FORM

> natura inventata

TRAVEL TREASURES A WORKER'S COTTAGE
GAVE A SYDNEY GALLERY OWNER A BLANK
CANVAS ON WHICH TO LEAVE HER MARK.
WITH BOLD ARTWORKS, 1960S CERAMICS
AND ASIAN TEXTILES, IT'S A TESTAMENT
TO HER TWO PASSIONS: ART AND TRAVEL

KEEP BRIGHT, GLAREY YELLOWS AS THE SMALL DETAIL RATHER THAN AS THE FOCUS IN A ROOM. TEAM THEM WITH SOFAS COVERED IN BLACK, DARK NAVY AND CHOCOLATE. DEEP YELLOWS THAT ARE LESS GLAREY CAN COPE BETTER AS THE BASE PALETTE.

Any aspect can benefit from bright yellow; rooms bathed in sunlight will keep the colour looking upbeat, and using it in a darker room can make the space appear lighter. If you love yellow but are after a more subdued effect, the softer, more low-key tones are ideal as the base in a room. Pale lemons work well as a wall-covering, either through paint or combined in a pattern in wallpaper to create a soft, pretty aesthetic. The more floral you go, the more traditional the effect; this is an ideal approach if you are living with classical architecture. Muted tones such as mustard and maize will create a warm, all-encompassing feel, and combining them with other spicy tones such as dusty reds and burnt oranges will result in an exotic flavour. In fact, mustard is a great tone

with which to colour the walls or upholster the furniture, or to use as flooring. You can use it as a base tone or an accent and it works just as well in a traditional as a contemporary space. Although not as cheery as the canary shades, mustard makes for a great all-rounder — although your room does need to hold a certain amount of light to prevent the colour from looking overly dull. Unlike the brighter shades, mustard tones work well in restful rooms such as bedrooms. Paired with a colour like chocolate, mustard will make your bedroom appear luxurious and decadent. The more zingy counterparts to the muted tones should be kept for action rooms only. Of course, the more opulent shades of gold are ideal for creating a dramatic effect, and work beautifully with silks and brocades. Ideally used as an accent rather than as the base, gold should be kept to a deep, rather than bright, shade to ensure its modernity.

YELLOW WORKS WITH ...

Colours that bring its brightness down a notch or two, such as chocolate or pale grey. The more muted shades combine well with grape and plum tones.

YELLOW WORKS WHERE ...

Kitchens are ideal for yellow's perpetual optimism. Touches in the lounge room will keep the space feeling alive. Playrooms benefit too.

pink Magenta Shell Strawberry Rose Fairy Floss Bubblegum Blossom Fuchsia Peony

WITH ITS FEMININE NATURE, PINK NATURALLY BELONGS IN A LITTLE GIRL'S ROOM. LAYER DIFFERENT TONES FOR INTEREST. FROM BLOSSOM TO MAGENTA, TO PINKS MIXED WITH MAUVE. TAKE IT OUT OF THE BEDROOM FOR AN UNEXPECTED TWIST IN SPACES SUCH AS THE LOUNGE ROOM AND DINING ROOM.

Feeling 'blue', down in the dumps or perhaps a little stressed out by life? Well, you've come to the right colour. Known as the great nurturer, pink will coax you through life's little difficulties; just a glimpse of this wonderful tone promotes feelings of caring, comfort and even sedation. Pink is the peacemaker, calming even the most aggressive among us with its gentleness; from tough men to tiny babies, no one could deny the physical benefits of immersing yourself in pink. Who could resist it?

Although it seems as though pink has always been a part of our cultural aesthetic, in reality pink only rose to prominence in the 1950s, when it became the colour of the moment. Elsa Schiaparelli designed the iconic 'shocking' pink ball gown, and the great Diana Vreeland, formidable editor of *Vogue,* announced that she adored pink as 'it's the navy blue of India!', securing pink's place in fashion heaven. Women were swathed in it and houses were dipped in it and Avon ladies in pink pillbox hats reaped the benefits as pink lipstick became the 'choix de vie' — everyone succumbed to the charm of pink. Even though we're living in a new millennium our passion for pink has not waned. Yes, it comes in and out of fashion in the expected cycles; but it never really falls from grace like most other colours in the spectrum do.

Traditionally seen as a feminine colour — although it does jump the fence from time to time — pink will always be associated with little girls' dresses and babies' rooms. The tranquillity of the palest of pinks induces a sense of calm and sleepiness; a benefit not lost on new parents the world over, battling sleepless nights. There's a sweetness to pale pink that you won't find in any other colour, which prompts in us feelings of innocence and memories of a time when life was just a little more simple.

Ramp the colour up a little though by adding less white and more red, and everything starts to change! Hotter shades of pink can result in an adrenaline jolt and a racing heartbeat; perfect if you need a little shock therapy, or even better, a little passion in your life. Wild, sexy and hot, hot, hot — brighter shades of pink such as magenta, fuchsia and scarlet all evoke feelings of high-intensity emotion. Conjuring images of women in hot pink underwear or the perfect hot pink pout, the brighter pinks have an impact similar to that of red, leaving us in a flurry of excitement — except that when it comes to pink, there's no doubt that its passion is totally feminine. Yes, pink is all woman — us girls have claimed it as our own. The power of pink is as much a symbol of the power of female sexuality — that is, it's sensual, sexy and ready for romance — as it is a colour to dress in or to use as a decorating tool for your home.

VOYAGEURS PASSE · VOYAGEURS DEBOUT
RAUCHEN
VERBOTEN

we love little peach!
we are peach boy kokeshi furuhol

motaro, little peach boy 'l our li

ABOVE: 'Montserrat' fabric by Manuel Canovas from C
Cooper. BELOW: floral fabric wall hanging from Newt
BOTTOM: Marimekko 'Ananas' fabric from Chee Soon &

ABOVE: photograph by Cora from Bloom magazine. OPPOSITE: Wooden
chair and 1950s still-life by Vladimir Naiditch from Manning &
Manning. 'Popkapu' fabric by Manuel Canovas from Geraldine Cooper.
Chinese chests and woven basket from Imagine This. Boat from Orson & Blake. Silk tassle
from Imagine This. Boat from Jodo's Beach House.
palm tree. Wooden 'palm' fram

But does that mean that you can only decorate in pink if you're living in a house full of girls? What if you love it regardless and need a little of it to get through your day? Is it possible to incorporate pink into a masculine space, or one shared with a masculine other half, without it looking overly girly and prissy, and without him feeling like he's being forced to go and live in the corridor? Of course, anything is possible, but for the sake of happy cohabitation there are a few things to consider. First of all, it's probably a good idea in this situation to save the chintzy shabby chic florals for a little girl's bedroom and the less-frequented areas of the home — perhaps your home office or workroom or, if you're lucky enough to have one, the summer house, as pink and florals combined push the feminine to the limit. The best approach is to keep the pinks to hotter or bluer shades and only infuse them in block colours — no pretty patterns. Sofa or floor cushions are a great idea to add just a taster of pink without it becoming overkill. A corner armchair that's not the focus of the room could cope as well, as could a lampshade or a small rug. If you can't resist a pattern, keep it geometric. Stripes are ideal, as are block shapes. Oriental patterns, where pink makes only a subtle appearance, work well. Always pair your pinks with stronger, more masculine, shades to take the girly edge off. Chocolate brown is a perfect match, as are neutrals with some intensity: deep navy blues and aubergine and grape colours. Avoid other 'electric' shades, such as limes and aqua blues, unless of course you thrive in a bright environment. Naturally, if you can't resist a floral, then keep it to a minimum — a single cushion paints a thousand words!

'I ADORE THAT PINK!'
IT'S THE NAVY BLUE OF INDIA!'

DIANA VREELAND

If the paler pinks are your thing but you want them to look modern and not too feminine, then again, it's a good idea to limit the colour to the accessories: a mohair throw rug, linen cushions, a collection of ceramics perhaps. Keep the colours solid, steering clear of pretty designs. Avoid the saccharine baby pastels and go for shades of shell and peony instead. In fact, sometimes a glass jar filled with soft pink shells or a vase filled with pale pink peonies is enough pink to make an impact. Bathrooms are an ideal place for it; adding fluffy towels, candles and bath salts in a range of pale pinks gives you a taste without you having to live with them permanently on display. Just bring them out when the pink bug bites. And don't forget the dusty tones, which combine beautifully with other muted shades to create a touch of Moroccan flavour at home. Whichever way you go and whichever pink you choose, you can be sure that pink will always be there for you, supporting and nurturing you in times of trouble.

PINK WORKS WITH ...

Orange for some razzamatazz! Purple for an Indian infusion. Other tones of pink are ideal if you're after a girly perspective. Chocolate brown will add a sense of maturity.

PINK WORKS WHERE ...

Naturally, in little girls' rooms. However, touches of pink go well in either the grown-ups' bedroom or the bathroom, depending on the shade.

blue

Azure **Aqua** **Electric** Cornflower Royal Turquoise **Cobalt** Sea Navy Sky

[SENSEOFSTYLECOLOUR]

BECAUSE OF THE RELAXING QUALITIES OF BLUE, A ROOM CAN COPE WITH BEING AWASH WITH EVEN THE MOST INTENSE SHADE. HERE, THE BLUE OF THE WALLS AND THE BLUE IN THE COLLECTION OF PORCELAIN WARE PLAY AN EQUAL PART IN THE DECOR, TO MAGICAL EFFECT.

'I NEVER GET TIRED OF THE BLUE SKY.'

VINCENT VAN GOGH

If it's at all possible for a colour to be considered a blessing, then there's no question that blue is it. We are so fortunate to be graced by this colour; every day its presence in the beaming blue sky and the deep blue of the ocean reminds us of how lucky we are to be alive. It's such an obvious symbol of vitality; when the sky is cloudless and the sun is shining we are reassured that life is thriving. Sunny days by the seaside; picnicking under clear skies in the park or out in the country; boating on a lake or harbour — all of these experiences are further enriched by the presence of blue. Even when the sky is cloudy, the possibility that a blue sky is hiding behind the grey is enough to spur us on. I remember how as a child I would float star-fish style in the ocean and look up at the sky — suspended carefree between two blues; how the ocean would support me from below and the blue sky would inspire me from above, making me smile. Blue is the colour that many of us hold most dear — its sentimental value is enough to provoke a swell of emotion. It is no wonder that it has been aligned with theology and spirituality throughout the ages and across cultures: the Virgin Mary has been immortalized in blue robes; in Judaism blue signifies holiness; and for the Chinese it symbolizes immortality.

Blue is considered to be a colour of the mind rather than the body, and as such it affects us mentally rather than physically. Just as soothing aromatherapy oil can calm the senses through smell, the colour blue can soothe via the sense of sight. Blue relaxes the mind and refines our ability to concentrate. Colour therapists say it helps to free us of erroneous thought and induce a flow of positivism. Because of this, it promotes communication and connectedness and as a result an increase in productivity and efficiency. If you need to get something done, but lack focus, dip into some blue for a quick burst of enthusiasm. It won't affect you powerfully, the way say, red or orange will, but it will facilitate clear thought.

The flip-side is that some shades can you leave you feeling blue — that is, cold, dejected and a little depressed. Too much meditation and not enough action can induce a cycle of self-reflection that can lead to . . . dare I say it . . . self-indulgence and self-pity! The painter Pablo Picasso's 'blue period' was symbolic of this state of mind. Blues music is an auditory version. Someone who is 'black and blue' is suffering from bruising and injury. Generally it is the cooler blues, the greyer tones with less red in the mix, that make us shiver. If you stick with the brighter interpretations instead of the icy hues, you are sure to keep your space upbeat. The wonderful aspect of blue is that it is very compliant and works in most spaces. Although traditionally seen as a colour only for boys, blue now crosses the line and works in either a feminine or masculine arena. There are so many hues with so many connotations that there is bound to be a blue that has resonance for each of us. My favourite is aqua blue, as it evokes memories of my time swimming in the warm Caribbean many years ago. Yours may be a warmer tone: a blue infused with an element of red.

Blue works well in most rooms, but is particularly effective in spaces that lend themselves to meditation and calmness or cleansing. The bathroom is an obvious place to employ it. Is there anything more enticing than a bathing space wrapped in blue mosaic tiles? It doesn't matter which shade — it could be anything from bright aqua and turquoise to deep shades of midnight — spending time in a space such as this allows you to reconnect with your inner self and leaves you in a state of pure tranquillity. Even touches of blue in an otherwise non-blue bathroom are enough to add a sense of calm: just add towelling and accessories to evoke the feel of the ocean.

PUT ALL TONES OF BLUE TOGETHER OR COUPLE WITH GREEN FOR A HARMONIOUS INTERIOR. ADD INTEREST BY INFUSING FIERY COLOURS SUCH AS RED AND ORANGE THROUGH THE DETAIL— EVEN A

The bedroom is another space that lends itself completely to blue. It's the one area that can cope with everything from blue-painted walls to a luxuriously blue-dressed bed. In the bedroom, you can give yourself over to the meditative qualities of the colour, and if you do it is sure to leave you feeling like you are floating on a sea of calm. I would recommend brighter and warmer shades of blue over the cooler shades, to prevent the room from appearing too cold; however, if you live in a space that is flooded by daylight and sunshine, this natural warmth will counteract any coolness. Although I have seen a lot of blue kitchens that work beautifully on an aesthetic level, you should think carefully if you are planning this option for your own home. If, like me, your kitchen is a flurry of activity, and you like it that way, then blue and its meditative qualities could leave you a little too relaxed for your own good. Touches of blue, however, won't have too much of an anaesthetic effect.

Most blues work well together in a mix. The deepness of dark blue is offset by the brightness of a turquoise highlight. Grey blues combine with pretty, lighter shades, and bold cobalt blues work well with powdery hues. Unlike the more dominant shades of red, orange and even purple, an all-blue room in its varying shades won't be offensive. Even so, it works beautifully in a combination; for example, coupled with the simplicity of white for a seaside feel and with the textural tones of oatmeal and natural linen for a more sophisticated twist. It also lives happily alongside its cousins, purple and green (both created with a mix of blue), as well as bluer shades of pink. Blue is a great all-rounder. Whatever the layout of a space, and its aspect to the sun, a blue exists that can work harmoniously there.

BLUE WORKS WITH ...

Blue and white is a fresh combination. Blue and green will put you in a meditative mood, and in touch with your inner self. Blue and red will give you an injection of spirit.

BLUE WORKS WHERE ...

Where doesn't blue work? Try it in the kitchen, playroom, bedroom, lounge room or in the bathroom. Blue is the great all-rounder.

brown Chocolate
Caramel Cappuccino Cocoa
Earth Ebony Almond Tan

BROWN IS A COMFORTING COLOUR; IT CONNECTS US WITH THE EARTH, MAKING US FEEL GROUNDED. HOWEVER, DON'T OVERDO IT. PAIRING LIGHT BROWNS WITH DARK CHOCOLATES AGAINST A BACKGROUND OF WHITE CREATES RICHNESS, WHILE RETAINING EASE AND A SENSE OF SPACE.

Willie Wonka had the right idea when he defined his life by the pursuit of creating the perfect chocolate! Although outwardly indulgent, at its core chocolate represents for us a deep sense of comfort and intimacy — two characteristics that we all require to help make the day-to-day of living a little more pleasant. In an odd way, the consumption of chocolate, even just a square, facilitates a connection to our inner selves, to the warmth of the familiar. If you're a devourer of chocolate, then no doubt you understand that deep feeling of satisfaction that you experience after a session of munching. The feeling that, yes, the world is as it should be and I can get on with my day!

Health enthusiasts would probably argue that you shouldn't need chocolate to feel at peace with your soul — but as a devotee myself, I say why not enjoy this sumptuous indulgence in one of god's gifts? Life without chocolate is a life less lived!

In the same way that chocolate affects us through our sense of taste, the colour brown affects us through our sense of sight. A mere glimpse of this wonderfully luscious and delectable colour will leave you feeling warm and cosy on the inside, completely at peace with the world and at one with yourself. Brown is, after all, one of the commonest colours in nature, along with green, and is manifested in the foundation of life itself: the sustaining earth beneath our feet. In many ways, life without brown would be just that little bit more tenuous.

Brown provides a sense of consistency that allows us to infuse it, in all of its incarnations, into our home environment: it is a very reliable colour to decorate with. More forgiving than black, but still deep and rich enough to provide a substantial backdrop, it should never be overlooked as a decorating option — but be careful how you use it. Just as brown is the colour of the earth, of the foundation of nature, in decorating it should be used as a base rather than to provide touches of fancy in a space. Read: don't go overboard! If you use only brown in your home — and this includes its paler versions such as beige and taupe — you run the risk of your space becoming bland, heavy and downright dull.

Pure Silk
3Yds (2.74m) 100%
Blue #126

7mm 7mm 7mm 7mm
Ribbon Embroidery
Bucilla
Made in China
Bucilla Corp. Hazleton, PA 18201

Of course, brown comes in many forms, from the deep, rich darkness of chocolate to the brighter, auburn shades and the warm, inviting caramels. Which shade you go for depends very much on the look that you are trying to achieve and, as always, the space that you are decorating. Made from a mix of black and yellow, brown takes on the same characteristics as its ingredients and so you should think about the effects that these individual colours have when choosing the right shade for you. Not only do you have a lighter shade of brown the more yellow you add, but you also have a colour with a sunnier disposition; think caramel. Because of the element of yellow in caramel it automatically adds energy to a room. Caramel works particularly well in darker spaces that aren't flooded with much direct sunlight, because it already has an inbuilt 'bounce'. However, avoid these yellowy shades of brown if you live in a space that's already flooded with loads of yellow natural light, as it will end up looking glarey. Add less yellow and the result is a richer but more sombre tone of dark chocolate, perfect if you live in a light-filled house — not so great if you live in a dark box as it will do nothing to uplift the space. Add a touch of feisty red and you have a vibrant shade of auburn that works well in any space.

The feel that you are trying to achieve should be your guide when choosing your tone: chocolate being more sophisticated, caramel more relaxed and auburn more energetic. Choose earthy tones to create a sense of stability and balance. The more neutral shades of taupe and beige create a sense of harmony and calm, adding more sophistication and depth than if you were to choose just plain white. My favourite shade of the bunch would have to be chocolate; not only because of its connection with my preferred food indulgence but because you can choose almost any colour as a highlight tone and it will work well. I have teamed my

TOO MUCH BROWN WILL CHOKE ANY ENVIRONMENT, LEAVING YOU FEELING STIFLED. REMEMBER THAT BROWN SHOULD MERELY BE THE FOUNDATION, THE BASE LAYER. ADD CONTRASTING COLOURS IN THE DECORATION.

'CHOCOLATE GIVES ONE THE FEELING OF BEING IN LOVE.'

WILLIE WONKA, CHARLIE AND THE CHOCOLATE FACTORY

chocolate linen sofa with a burnt orange shag pile rug and bright green chair, and somehow the blend works well. However, anything from bright or mustard shades of yellow, to pink, aqua or mauve pair beautifully with this wonderful tone. Different shades of brown can work well together in a room, but generally keep this mixing for the accessories. Stick with the same shade of brown in the wooden pieces of furniture that make up the foundation of your room, otherwise you will create a real mish-mash when you add layers of differently coloured accessories. Too many colours in a room will cancel each other out. As I mentioned earlier, avoid going overboard with your use of brown to ensure that it stays relevant — it's best kept for the main or grounding pieces of furniture in a room: a sofa, coffee or dining table or a rug.

BROWN WORKS WITH …

Brown supports almost every other shade from the colour wheel. Choose deep muted shades of yellow and orange over the brighter versions. However, hot pink and bright blue pair well.

BROWN WORKS WHERE …

Definitely in the lounge room and bedroom for a sense of connection to the earth and a sophisticated aesthetic.

base colours Jet

Ink Charcoal Dove Milk Chalk

BASE TONES — THAT IS, BLACK, WHITE AND GREY — BY DEFINITION ARE DEVOID OF COLOUR. BUT LOOK CLOSELY AND YOU'LL SEE THEY HAVE A PERSONALITY OF THEIR OWN. THEIR MANY NUANCES CAN HELP YOU ACHIEVE A RICHLY LAYERED INTERIOR.

black...

'BLACK IS A FORCE.' *HENRI MATISSE*

It's not easy to be colourful when black is present. Its very nature signifies a lack of humour and an inability to see the light side of life. Because of this it tends to take over — when black is around there's not much room for anything else, and so using black in an interior isn't for the faint-hearted. Only those who are brave enough to live with such a powerful presence in their homes should delve into its depths. However, if you are one of the brave, and have the strength to stand up to its persuasiveness, then black can be very rewarding as it makes for a unique and dramatic aesthetic.

Black has very definite connotations in our culture and our psyche. It represents a sense of foreboding and mystery; it makes us aware of danger, as it signifies menace and evil. It is the symbol of death and destruction. Black is an outcast to some degree, denoting secrecy and morbidity. Darth Vader, the black-clad villain from *Star Wars*, is an apt personification — as are Dracula and the Wicked Witch of the West. On the other hand, black evokes a sense of sophistication, confidence and glamour. In terms of the colour spectrum, black is created through the absorption of all light in the same way that white is created through the reflection of light: in this way it is all encompassing, and has come to be seen as a symbol of authority in many societies. Black is a protector of sorts: once it casts its cloak around you, you become mesmerized by its power. However, it is not always reassuring; in fact, the effect that black creates is almost eerie. Picture the mafia, in their black suits and cars. Powerful yes; but also sinister! Although we derive some sense of strength from this colour, it is a tenuous strength, and one that leaves us with the feeling of wariness.

Yet despite all of this, black can be a wonderful colour to use in an interior, and it works particularly well as a highlight colour. Give it too much power and it takes complete control. Use it as a modest presence only, so it can't take over. The tone of black you use, whether it is dense or permeable, very much depends on the texture of the material that you are using it on, and will affect the look that you are trying to achieve. If you choose a dense shade, in a deep velvet or silk, it will create a sense of sophistication and glamour. Anything with sheen to it makes black look very chic and luxurious. Black linen, however, with its coarse texture, will produce a more relaxed ambience: the loose weave of the linen creates a muted, almost washed-out effect, dulling the impact and making black a great choice for a sofa or armchair. Black-lacquered furniture makes for a highly formal setting. Black floorboards paired with white walls create a zen environment.

What is wonderful about black is that it does work well with almost every other colour of the spectrum. Choose reds and oranges for an upmarket, Eastern flavour. Pair yellow and black for a chic, 1960s inspired Marimekko or Florence Broadhurst feel. Add pink for some quirky glamour. My favourite combination would have to be textured black fabrics paired with shades of walnut, chocolate, burnt orange and muted greens, which when all put together seem to capture the essence of Africa. It's a wonderfully relaxed arrangement, and although the black has a presence in this environment its more muted tone ensures that it works well as part of larger group.

It goes without saying that black's most natural partner is of course white. The depth of the black offsets the luminosity of the white and makes for a wonderful marriage. An all-white warehouse space filled with classically designed 1950s-style furniture makes a statement that is impossible to ignore. If you are after dramatic effect in your space, the combination of black and white is the glamour couple. And the effect is sure to be noticed.

My main message here is to avoid creating a black hole by completely blanketing your space with it. Subtlety is the key. Always ensure that you pair it with another more uplifting colour to be certain that your space won't feel cavernous and overly depressing.

BLACK WORKS WITH ...

White, of course! However, for a little more oomph, try it with hot shades of pink and bright shades of yellow. Pair with neutrals for an eclectic flavour. Red will create an Asian feel.

BLACK WORKS WHERE ...

In lounge room furnishings, paired with white on the kitchen or bathroom floor, and in the kitchen for those who eat out a lot. Spare the bedroom.

white...

'WHITE . . . IS NOT A MERE ABSENCE OF COLOUR,
IT IS A SHINING AND AFFIRMATIVE THING
AS FIERCE AS RED, AS DEFINITIVE AS BLACK. . .'
G.K. CHESTERTON

WHO SAYS WHITE IS BLAND? PREVENT WHITE FROM LOOKING CLINICAL BY USING IT SIMPLY AS A BACKDROP OR CANVAS ON THE WALLS AND FLOORS OF YOUR HOME. THEN OVERLAY IT WITH A RICH, NATURAL PALETTE TO PROVIDE WARMTH AND DEPTH.

If there is a heaven on earth, white may just be as close as we get to it. After all, it is considered the purest colour of them all; there is no other colour — or reflection of light in this case — that conjures up visions of angels and fluffy clouds quite like white does. Its luminosity is so endearing. Maybe it's because of this that white has become a religious and cultural symbol, representing purity of soul and divinity. In the Christian faith, babies are christened in white dresses and women are swathed in white gowns at their marriage to represent their chasteness and commitment to god. Those who claim that they've 'been to the other side' talk of being drawn towards 'a white light'. Hospital doctors wear sterile white robes. A white dove denotes peace and purity of spirit.

In the same way that white represents innocence in a cultural sense, it evokes a feeling of purity when used in interiors. When we sink into an all-white interior we experience a feeling of relaxation and tranquillity, as though we were resting on a cloud. The reflection of light emanating from white is almost ethereal; spending time in such an environment will leave you feeling more at peace with yourself. Because of this, white is often used to decorate holiday spaces such as beach houses and environments that need to evoke a feeling of restfulness. Naturally, bathrooms, the rooms we use to purify our bodies and our souls, are often all white. White is a popular colour for kitchens, providing a sense of cleanliness and hygiene.

The flip-side is that white can come across as being overly sterile and unfriendly. The traditional image of the all-white psychiatric hospital has encouraged the idea that spending too much time in an all-white space can be bad for your mental health. The white straitjacket symbolizes a loss of freedom, extreme restraint. There's nothing like a bit of colour to inspire the mind and the body.

Although we tend to think of all whites as being one and the same, in truth there are many tonal variations, and you will find that each one creates a slightly different effect. Simply flicking through a catalogue at your local paint shop will prove to you that not all whites are created equal. You will find everything from bright white to chalk white, yellow whites and blue whites: each will create a different mood, depending on the space in which it is employed. Stark white is a confrontational shade that will have light bouncing around a room — there's nowhere to hide in a stark white space. Warm whites soften the outlook a little, taking on a yellow tone, creating warmth and comfort.

Blue tones are icy and cold — perfect for a warm climate. Pink whites add a touch of femininity minus the girliness. Many of us choose white simply due to a lack of inspiration; white is the decorating fall guy. However, it can't be denied that white makes for a great base in a room, particularly on the walls. All-white walls are the perfect backdrop for an art collection, and this background scheme is a benign player when you are seeking to use bright colour in your upholstery. Paired with a coloured feature wall it's sure to make a statement.

WHITE WORKS WITH ...

White is everybody's friend and as such pairs beautifully with all colours of the spectrum. Blue and green particularly can cope with a larger dose.

WHITE WORKS WHERE ...

Where doesn't white work? The kitchen and bathroom are the obvious choices. Use it on the walls and the floors throughout a floorboarded interior, as well as in the furnishings. Create interest by pairing your whites with lush textures in your upholstery.

BLACK, WHITE AND GREY IN GRAPHIC SHAPES MAKE A POWERFUL COMBINATION.

grey...

'IF I SEE EVERYTHING IN GREY, AND IN GREY ALL THE COLOURS WHICH I EXPERIENCE AND WHICH I WOULD LIKE TO REPRODUCE, THEN WHY SHOULD I USE ANY OTHER COLOUR?' *ALBERTO GIACOMETTI*

Poor old grey. Grey lives in no-man's land, lying somewhere between the power of black and the purity of white. It's a sad colour, evoking a sense of dullness, denoting a lack of freedom. There's no doubt about it, grey days are dull days and the very essence of the colour is kind of chilly, don't you think? Wild grey oceans; grey storm clouds; grey faces — it seems to be the pessimist of the colour world! But not always: from a decorating perspective, grey is, in fact, a very malleable tone to use. Grey works in a way that neither the boldness of black nor the starkness of white allows. It is a kind of filler, if you like. Grey is the quiet achiever — it can round out an interior, giving it a sense of substance, without drawing too much attention to itself. This colour has no ego; it is happy to step aside and let other colours shine, doing the hard yards as the support instead. Use grey in your home to create a calm, cool base for a brighter shade. Nothing evokes the sense of the ocean like a home decorated in a combination of grey with white highlights. Grey combined with bright yellow creates energy, and grey with pink allows the pink to stand out front, but not alone.

As always, it's all about where you use it to get the best effect. Grey coupled with cold, wild weather will only make you shiver, so greys are generally recommended for warmer climates. If you live in a cool climate, but can't live without grey, then make sure you pair it with a warmer tone to add heat. Grey is perfect for the bedroom or the living room if you want to create a calm environment. Forget the bathroom though, as the essence of grey can look grubby — not good for a cleansing space. Grey in the kitchen, through the use of stainless steel, adds a professional touch, but steer clear of grey in the tilework — grubby again!

Of course, grey comes in many tones: as you darken the effect, moving through to charcoal tones, the grey takes on many of the attributes of black, including absorbing the light. By contrast, light greys take on many of white's better attributes, reflecting light and creating a sense of space. I love pale grey floors coupled with white walls and beachy linen furnishings, Hamptons style. The lightness of the combination is uplifting and heartening — not the effect that you would normally expect from poor old grey.

GREY WORKS WITH ...

Black and white are its obvious first cousins; however, be adventurous and pair grey with bright yellow or pink as both are complemented by the neutrality of grey.

GREY WORKS WHERE ...

Steer clear of bathrooms and kitchens. Stick to lounge and dining areas and perhaps use a smattering in the bedroom. Outdoor furniture benefits greatly from grey.

Sa anticipare la moda e suggerire nuovi scenari domestici. Andrea Dall'Olio per lavoro vive nel futuro, ma nel privato non si sottrae al fascino del passato

di Rosaria Zucconi · foto di Max Zambelli

ECCESSI DECORATIVI

03
creating
with
colour

CREATING YOUR OWN SENSE OF STYLE IS ABOUT COMBINING YOUR PERSONAL RESPONSES TO COLOUR WITH A SOUND UNDERSTANDING OF THE ELEMENTS OF DESIGN.

colour your world

Only when you open your eyes to the interplay of colour with various environments – both natural and built – and connect with your reactions, can you start to define your colour aesthetic.

In Chapter 1, I aimed to move you a step closer to really seeing the colour around you. Once you have become aware of how and where to find inspiration, it's time to go further along the path of your colour journey, to see how you personally react to specific colours, and that is hopefully what you've taken from Chapter 2. At the end of the day, you want the colour in your home to serve you to some degree; to help inspire in you a reaction — whether that be one of calm or excitement is up to you. You are the only judge here. As much as we all want our friends and loved ones to add weight to our choices with their approval, ultimately, if the colour is not doing it for you, then it's of no use!

So then, where to from here? Now that you're armed with a true sense of yourself and the colours you feel most comfortable living with, it's time to put the process into practice. It's one thing having a good grasp of colour but it's another to employ your knowledge in your home. Throwing colour around the place, with no sense of direction or reason, does not a pretty place make. It is important to combine the creativity of colour with an understanding of the principles of good design — the two go hand in hand, something like a good marriage. Creativity without boundaries makes for a creative collision; but too many boundaries make for constraint and lack of excitement. It is a fine balance of colour, design and personality that creates an interesting home. Although the principles of design represent the tried

DON'T ISOLATE THE PROCESS OF COLOUR DISCOVERY FROM COLOUR APPLICATION WHEN MAKING YOUR CHOICES. THE TWO SHOULD BE EQUALLY WEIGHTED IN YOUR MIND. ONLY WHEN YOU COMBINE THE BEAUTY OF COLOUR WITH SHAPE AND FORM CAN YOU ACHIEVE YOUR DESIRED AESTHETIC.

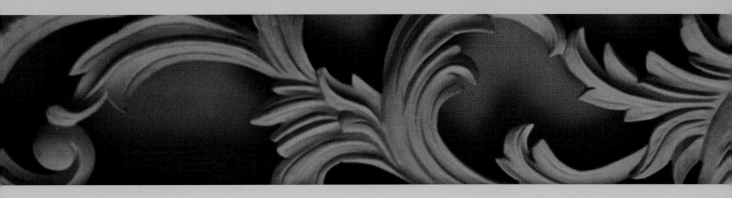

'NEXT COMES THE MATERIAL . . . AND OUT OF THIS COMES, OF COURSE, THE COLOUR – AND, IN SUM, THE OVERALL IMPRESSION.' *ARNE JACOBSEN*

and true approach to creating a harmonious environment, I hope that you won't allow the 'rules' to inhibit you in any way. The purpose here is to create an environment that is individual and eclectic, and sometimes that means going against the rules altogether. However, I do believe that before you can revolutionize design you first need a grasp of what it is that you are revolutionizing. In the same way that many of our most radical artists have a sound knowledge of the breadth of their art before they start pushing the envelope, it's important to have a good sense of the design basics before you turn design on its head.

Once you have grasped the basics of interior design — have a bit of fun with them. Experiment; think of it as a personal project. Work in stages, layering your work. If at first you don't like what you see, alter, massage and develop it until you get it as you want it. Like all areas of creativity developing an interior is a lengthy process. It's worth the time and energy because at the end you will be comfortable with your choices, and as a result will hopefully live with them longer. Although the one-stop shopping approach to decorating fills a momentary need, it also falls prey to the whims of fashion. Before you know it, you'll be over it and the whole process will have to start again, which is a time-consuming and costly process for anyone. Take your time, enjoy yourself and create a space you feel at one with.

know your space

Your personal response to colour is a vital part of the design process – fusing colour with your existing space to create a harmonious whole is another.

No doubt you're feeling some sense of accomplishment and excitement at having unearthed a sense of colour and a palette that works for you. Becoming aware of colour and how you relate to it is in some ways a journey of discovery, and with any new discovery comes some sense of satisfaction.

However, before you head out to the shops and invest in a whole new colour scheme, it's important to reflect on the environment for which these new colours are intended. In the same way that it's important to dress your body in colours that you love but which also suit your skin tone and body shape, it's important to dress your home in colours that suit the space they are meant for.

So, as is always my approach, I recommend you stop for a while, take a seat and have a good look at the space where you spend much of your life. Have you ever really noticed how the rooms operate from a practical perspective? Most of us are guilty of filling our homes with the required amount of furniture and then never really thinking about the interior again. In order to create an environment where you feel at peace, it's vital to know how that space operates on a daily basis and how you function within it. Become aware of the floor plan of the room that you are focusing on and ask yourself a few questions about its interior. Is it a large or small room? Is it square, rectangular or irregular? Is there much free wall space or are the walls taken up with storage or windows? How does this room flow onto the next space? Is it open plan or completely enclosed? How does the natural light move through the room as the day progresses? Are you living in the dark for most of the day or are you assaulted by excessive amounts of sunlight? Each individual issue that your room presents to you requires a certain response to ensure that your space is secured by a firm foundation.

It is likely that the interiors you admire most have a strongly defined layout and a respect for how that layout works. Room layout is the foundation that grounds your space; decoration and embellishment provide the energy. Without a solid foundation, the embellishment simply seems trivial; the foundation has to be in place before the fun can begin.

USE COLOUR AS A TOOL TO HELP YOU CREATE BALANCE AND SYMMETRY IN YOUR SPACE. THIS ALL-TURQUOISE CHEST OF DRAWERS CREATES A SOLID FOUNDATION FOR THE MULTITUDE OF DETAILS AND COLOURS THAT REST ON IT.

BALANCE

In an ideal world our interiors would come prepackaged, in just the right shape — preferably square — punctuated by a couple of perfectly spaced windows situated in an aspect that perfectly captures the orientation of the sun. There would be balance and symmetry in the design, the space working as a kind of blank canvas to allow you to create to your heart's content. The reality, of course, is very different. Unless you are fortunate enough to be able to build a house from scratch — with your personal design requirements as the priority, you are, like most of us, stuck with what you get: somebody else's idea of how a space should be. Often that means oddly shaped rooms, unbalanced wall space and sun just where you don't need it! These kinds of problems are particularly prevalent in older buildings that were generally built before we became the design savvy bunch that we are now. One of the wonderful aspects of colour is that it can be a useful tool to unify even the messiest layout. It's important to think about not only the right colours for your space but also the means by which you infuse the colour into your space — whether that be paint, upholstery, artwork — as each element works to add a different quality to a room. Each room will require a different response; but ultimately what you are trying to achieve is a certain balance. Perhaps you can relate to some of the following problems.

NO NATURAL LIGHT

If your room is dark for most of the day, your aim will be to maximize the light that is available to you. There are two approaches that you can take. The first, a possibility for those happy to live in the dark, is to go with the flow rather than working against the lack of light. Create a 'boudoir' of sorts and choose deeply coloured, lushly textured fabrics to enrich the space and make it a cosy haven. Select from the family of red and go for rich chocolates, deep purple and grape tones, and red itself, of course. Paint the walls in tones of this rich palette. Use coloured candles and warm, golden lighting to maximize the atmosphere. Choose plush flooring with a pattern that combines all of the above colours to bring the space together. This look works particularly well if you live in a cooler climate, as the richness of the aesthetic will warm even the coldest environment.

However, if you love the sun and the feeling of being outdoors, this colour combination could leave you a touch depressed. In this case you need to use colours that pump up and reflect any available light. Painting the walls white is the most obvious course, but be careful which shade you employ as stark white can leave an already cold, dark room feeling icy. Use a warmer shade of white — that is, one infused with a touch of yellow — to add a little heat to the room. This creates a simple backdrop for a décor of pale linen furnishings in zingy shades of aqua, turquoise, yellow or green. Of course, white is not the only colour for your walls: you can use light and uplifting shades of pink or mauve as well; both contain an element of red which will add heat to a cold room. Keep it pale — but always energetic. This palette lends itself perfectly to geometric patterns in bright colours in the furnishings, which will instantly lift the mood. And don't forget that metallic paint colours work to dramatic effect if you're in need of some light. Stick to the paler shades of silver and pink and you're sure to have light bouncing around the room.

LIGHT IS TOO BRIGHT

If your space is flooded with natural light and you need to tone it down, avoid white at all costs. White is a reflective colour and a bright room painted white will be filled with glaring light, leaving you squinting. Stick to deeper colours that absorb the light — that applies to everything from the window treatments to the sofa covers. Go for cooler colours in shades of blue and green, as warm tones of red, orange and yellow will only serve to warm the space up further. Good-quality blinds and window treatments that are backed with an ultraviolet block-out will ensure your fabrics don't fade.

SMALL SPACE

Although the colour you use in a small room won't actually increase the available floor space, it will give the illusion that it has. In a small space colour works as a kind of mirage; it tricks the eye into thinking one thing when the reality is a much different story. If you do want to make a small room appear larger, the key is to keep the colours pale. And I mean really pale — read: almost white. Add to the expansiveness by painting the ceiling white to give the room a sense of height. Cover floorboards in a white paint or lime wash to maximize the effect; if you prefer natural wood, choose timbers in a washed-out tone. If you're living with carpet, choose a lighter shade. Going pale works not only for the paint colours on the walls but also for the furnishings. Lighter tones for your sofa, flooring and bed linen will keep the mood of the space upbeat. Also ensure that the fabric textures are light and breezy, as heavy-weight fabrics work to close a room in.

OVERSIZED AREA

The reverse situation, the scourge of modern design in my opinion, is the oversized, expansive open-plan living area. It seems that amid all the excitement about opening up our living spaces — combining kitchen, living and dining rooms — in the hope of creating a relaxed environment, we've been left with large, cold rooms that in reality don't promote intimacy or comfort. Where exactly do you plant yourself in an open-plan warehouse-style location to find cosiness and connection? Some of you may love this feeling of expansiveness in your home; however, if like me you want to add a sense of intimacy, choose darker colours that work to close in a room. To really add to the atmosphere, choose muted, spicy tones of brown, orange, yellow, red and purple. Although the dark versions from the cool colour palette of blue and green will work, they won't create the warmth that an oversized room requires. Add strength not only through the wall colour but also through the furnishings. Making a larger space more intimate is as much about placement of furniture as it is about colour, so create vignette areas throughout the middle of the space rather than attaching your pieces to the walls. Use strong colours that will give the effect of a reduction in dead space. Oversized rugs on the floor in intense shades give your furnishings a strong foundation. If you are living in a warm climate and could do with cooling off your space, go for a palette of blues and greens rather than the spicy red-based colours that will only work to create more heat.

ODDLY SHAPED ROOM

A room afflicted with an odd shape presents many difficulties — in fact, these rooms often seem almost impossible to decorate. Perhaps you have no wall space for hanging paintings. Or perhaps your space forms an L-shape; or there's an annoying little alcove that seems to be hanging out the side of the main room all on its lonesome. Or it could be that the windows are in all the wrong places. My favourite challenge is when one room just seems to spill into the next, providing no definition between two spaces and creating a nightmare if the two rooms serve completely opposing purposes. What to do? Well, again, the idea is to create some sense of balance. If your room has only slivers of wall — as is the case in many of the new high-rise apartment blocks — the last thing you want to do is to create a feature of the wall by using a dynamic, 'notice me' colour. Keep the backdrop simple, using a fairly neutral shade, and add colour through the furnishings. If your space is designed in an L-shape, maintain continuity by extending your palette throughout the whole space; you may choose a deeper, more prominent colour on the walls, which is an obvious sign that you are trying to unify the spaces. Keep the colour scheme flowing through the furnishings as well; a good tip to remember is that if you are choosing a prominent colour for the walls you should balance the rest of the furnishings with a 'subservient' tone, adding only touches of the dominant colour through the accents. If you are choosing a soft colour for the walls, you can afford some strength of colour in the furniture, and you can overlay accents of softness through your cushions and throws.

Mocking up a floor plan

It can be difficult for the naked eye to accurately visualize the concept of proportion and space in a room. However, to ensure that the space works harmoniously, it's important to get an idea of how the layout of your room and the furniture that you plan to place in it relate to one another. To gain a more concrete idea of how to apply colour to your particular space, draw a floor plan to scale, making sure to include the placement of your furniture and decorating detail. Alternatively, arrange some paper cutouts representing your furniture on a piece of paper, get out your pencils and colour the cutouts in the palette you are intending to use. Arrange them in a way that ensures balance and symmetry, and then mimic the layout in real scale.

[unearth the essence
of what you love
FLOWERS]

CHOOSE FLOWERS THAT ENHANCE THE COLOURS IN YOUR DECORATION. THESE BRIGHT RED BLOOMS FORM A VIBRANT AND GRAPHIC PARTNERSHIP WITH THE BLACK AND WHITE 1950S CHAIR AND SIDE TABLE.

Who could ignore the multitude of colour options found in flowers? The blood red in a rose or the subtlety of a pink peony, the delicate lilac of sweet peas, or the blues and purples of hydrangeas, the colours found in flowers can always be relied upon to stimulate the senses. I'm always woken from my winter-induced creative slumber when I see the first buds of jasmine weaving through my front fence — the way the soft pink buds bloom into little white flowers as the weather warms always arouses my senses. A visit to the local flower market is an experience sure to open your eyes to the colour opportunities that our floral world offers. A stroll through the botanical gardens works in the same way. And of course, seeing the beauty of flowers growing wild in a field, just as nature intended, reminds us that all the inspiration you need can be found there.

It makes sense to use flowers as the starting point for your colour palette. After all, it's one of the best ways to see vibrant, living colour at work. Notice how flowers in the field or in the garden change colour depending on the time of day and season; how cut flowers change from the moment they are snipped and popped into a vase to the end of their life. A cottage garden, with its mix of variety and colour, could be viewed as one large, living, breathing colour chart.

Would it be so odd to take your preferred type of rose to the paint shop and ask for a colour match, or to use your favourite shade of daisy as the springboard for your choice of upholstery fabric? Don't let convention hold you back when you are trying to unearth the essence of what you love — the most unique ideas are often born from eccentricity.

illumination

It's easy to underestimate the role that light plays in an interior and our colour choices for it.

We tend to pay it very little heed when making our choices about where and how we want to live. But in reality, light is the element of design that can have more influence on how you exist in your space than any other. Light affects us not only from a practical perspective — in that it illuminates our interior, helping us to manoeuvre ourselves around our home — but also from an emotional perspective. Whether it is natural or artificial, the role of light in our homes is to create atmosphere; and the kind of atmosphere that it creates can have a real influence on your general wellbeing. Stop and reflect on your reaction next time you find yourself underneath some harsh fluorescent lighting. Think about how you feel when you spend time in a place lacking any natural light. What impact does this have on your mood? I remember how depressed I was when, in my early twenties, I lived in Paris, holed up in an apartment that had no natural light at all. It was pitch black all day long — summer and winter. Imagine, depressed in Paris! Needless to say, I spent most of my time outdoors, which is generally how the locals prefer to live. Such is the significant role that light can play in your life.

With this in mind, having a strong sense of how light works in your interior is a must before you go about choosing colours to decorate with. Light and colour should never work in isolation. Always think about the amount of light that you receive and how the light changes during the day. A blue viewed early in the morning, when your home isn't receiving any direct sunlight, will appear as a different blue when seen by the light of the afternoon sun. That same blue will take on a different character when viewed under artificial lighting or lamp lighting. And yet again, the blue will take on a different tone when lit by different types of light bulbs. Light bulbs emitting a yellow glow will change the tone of your colour scheme completely: your blue, for example, will end up looking more of a green. Fluorescent tube lighting will leave it feeling cold and flat. Halogen lighting, which emits a white light, is the closest light to daylight available and as such is proving a popular choice as it keeps colours fairly true. If you have a lampshade covered in a coloured fabric, that will also affect the tone of the light. Remember that the direction in which your light source is facing will influence the effect.

LET THE SUN SHINE IN! HOW YOU REGULATE THE LIGHT WILL AFFECT THE COLOUR IN YOUR SPACE. SHUTTERS, WHICH FILTER LIGHT TO YOUR REQUIREMENTS, ARE ONE WAY TO MAKE SURE YOU GET THE BEST OF BOTH WORLDS.

[SENSE OF STYLE COLOUR]

AN ESSENTIALLY NEUTRAL PALETTE, WITH JUST A SMATTERING OF INTENSE COLOUR, WILL HELP YOU MAXIMIZE THE AVAILABLE LIGHT IN A ROOM. AT NIGHT, COSY UP THE COOLNESS OF IT ALL WITH CANDLELIGHT.

CHOREOGRAPHING LIGHT

How you regulate the available light in your home is also important. Plantation shutters, which control light without blocking it completely, will keep your colour as true as possible to its intended tone. Transparent blinds will merely cast a shadow over your colour scheme, dulling the tones slightly; whereas block-out blinds will deepen the colours immensely. It's important to acknowledge that light is a moveable feast. Natural light is never static: it is always moving, creating varying nuances in the colour and mood of our homes. Nor is the look of artificial lighting a 'given'. You can use dimmers, lamp lighting and candles to control the mood in your space. Lighting also affects the colours in your home, enhancing or dulling colour depending on how it's used. Why not use this to your advantage — by manipulating the lighting of your chosen colour palette you can enjoy the effect of two or three colour schemes; a colour scheme to match your every mood.

Try before you buy

Just as it's important for a woman to try her make-up on in natural light to ensure the trueness of the colours, so too is checking your intended interior colour scheme in natural light. When buying paint start by only purchasing a sample pot, and check the colour in daylight at the paint store to ensure you are getting the desired shade. Test the sample colour in its proposed position before you make any final decisions. This way you can be sure of how that tone works in your home throughout the day, before you go to the expense of making your final paint purchase. The same goes for your upholstery fabrics. Fabric stores are always happy to cut you a piece of sample cloth to try out at home, and you should take advantage of this service. In some cases, stores will allow you to take items of furniture (particularly easily moveable pieces such as chairs, rugs and lamps) home on a pro bono basis so that you can test the piece out in its intended space. Make use of this opportunity where you can as it will save you from investing in a piece of furniture and a colour scheme that don't suit your environment.

fixed colour

Think about applying colour to a room through a process of layering. Layer number one is the fixed colour, the backdrop to your space.

WALLS AND FLOORS

Now that you're conscious of how your fixed space works throughout the day, taking into account the balance of your room and the orientation of the sun, you can start to think about colouring that space. My approach is to think of the decoration of a room in terms of layers, starting out with the colours that actually form the space; that is, the shade of the paint, wallpaper or tilework that covers the walls and the flooring (whether that be carpeting or floorboards and so on). These are fixed colours, in that once you have made your choices you have to live with them; they cannot usually be altered without great expense. Of course, this is about the time that most home decorators start to feel the pressure. Making a mistake at this point can influence the rest of your decorating choices, and of course, wreak havoc on your self-esteem. Have faith, however: if you have a strong sense of your decorating loves, and have taken your time and done your research — and if you don't let fear get in the way — you will end up making the right choices. A few pointers are in order though.

PAINTED WALLS

I like to think of paint as the one aspect of your fixed space that you can change with relative ease and without crippling expense. And so it seems like the logical place to experiment with colour. Having said that, and without wanting to put a dampener on your creativity, it's important to think of your walls as the backdrop to your room rather than as the major player. Generally, wall space makes up a large component of any room, and so if you choose a dazzling, electric colour you're guaranteed that it will take over, drowning out all other aspects of decoration. As a result, the balance of your room will be 'off' — the effect will leave you feeling uncomfortable, at worst exhausted. That doesn't mean you can't go for a strong tone — I've seen rooms painted in a deep ocean blue or dusty aubergine work well (always rooms with loads of natural light); the subdued quality of these shades absorbs the emphasis, drawing attention away from the colour rather than towards it. Keep the ceilings white in this case to avoid creating a sense of oppression.

DON'T FORGET THAT PAINT COMES IN VARYING TEXTURES — FROM GLOSS TO MATT, LIME WASH TO METALLIC — AND EACH TEXTURE AFFECTS COLOUR DIFFERENTLY.

Ultra-bright, 'notice me' shades are best kept for a feature wall — that life-saving decorating device that allows us to delve into the world of crazy colour without having to be completely enveloped by it. I've painted one wall in my son's room a bright aqua blue — the other three walls are stark white. Painting the whole room aqua could just possibly have sent him, and me, over the edge, so this seems like a worthwhile compromise. Always choose the most prominent wall as your feature; a complete wall rather than a sliver works best for dramatic effect. Entrance areas work well as a canvas for feature colours, as does the area behind beds. Using colour in this way can achieve an additional effect, drawing the eye away from areas of the room that you want to camouflage, so choose your feature wall with this in mind. If you can't resist a zingy tone (such as cobalt blue, lime green or tomato red), keep it to activity areas such as kitchens and bathrooms. Please, though, just stick to one of these wild shades rather than going for the whole gamut . . . I can feel the onset of nausea just thinking about it!

Chalky, muted tones of sand make for a subtle backdrop, and the colour is more uplifting than a beige or taupe. I know how popular beige has become in contemporary interiors, and I'm not denying its benefit as a neutral, unobtrusive tone for the walls — but I can only really warm to it when it is paired with a colour with character. I've seen beige work beautifully as a backdrop to turquoise, grape, steel blue and dusty red. Without colour, beige just seems to be lacking in personality — it's just so . . . beige! Let's face it, even white has more attitude — and because it is also such a good all-rounder, and goes with practically anything, it has endeared itself to many a home renovator. Choose white only if you are living with natural light, get plenty of direct sun or intend to pair it with warm, cosy shades in your furnishings — otherwise your space will appear cold.

Pale, muted shades of blue, green and even grey make an ideal background, as their subtlety won't detract from your other furnishings. Being restful tones they make for a very relaxing environment. Baby pastels will leave your room looking twee, so steer clear of these tones except for babies' rooms (unless, of course, you love a bit of twee in your life).

THE BATHROOM IS AN IDEAL PLACE TO EXPERIMENT WITH BOLD COLOURS IN THE TILEWORK. AFTER ALL, IT IS THE MOST PRIVATE ROOM IN THE HOUSE.

WALLPAPER

Thank goodness that wallpaper has become fashionable again; I can't think of a more sophisticated way to infuse colour and pattern into a home. I view wallpaper as a kind of artwork for your walls, providing colour and interest for the eye and excitement for the soul. Sadly, though, many people are scared to use it — the permanency of the pattern and the fear that once it falls out of fashion you'll be stuck with it outweigh its benefits. The contemporary approach to wallpaper is to use it sparingly. Gone are the days when you'd wrap a whole room or, even worse, every room in the house in the stuff. These days decorators use it to cover a feature wall only — which could be anything from an entrance wall to a bedroom wall or a wall along the staircase. This way, although the wallpaper adds interest to a room, it doesn't take over and overwhelm the rest of the décor. Remember that if you are using a very colourful, highly patterned wallpaper, you will need to keep the rest of your furnishings fairly neutral, otherwise they'll all be competing for attention — which will ultimately cancel out the desired total effect. Wallpaper featuring more subtle colour combinations and a simpler design tends to balance and blend with stronger colours through the furnishings. In this case, choose the stronger colour from the pattern and use that as your base tone for the furniture. For wallpapers with a two-colour pattern, pick the subservient tone to decorate the bulk of your furniture, then use the dominant tone (and all its gradations) for the detail.

WALL TILES

Most people tend to keep the tiles on the walls of their kitchens and bathrooms to neutral shades of white or beige these days. I presume it's a cost factor; perhaps it's just fashion. In my opinion these are the two places where you can experiment with vivid colour. Generally the space to be covered is limited to either a splashback in the kitchen or the wet areas of the bathroom, and so should neither affect the cost too greatly nor overpower other aspects of the décor. As these spaces tend to be action rooms, they can cope with the energy of bold primary shades. An all-white kitchen with a bright-red-tiled splashback or a bright orange mosaic bathroom are sure to create a sense of energy and action. Bathrooms tiled completely in aqua and turquoise evoke a sense of relaxation and harmony. Midnight blue in the bathroom reminds us of the deep blue ocean. Wood-veneer kitchens coupled with milky green or pale mustard tiles look very sophisticated and grown up. Whatever you choose, this is your opportunity to have a bit of fun — let loose!

CARPET

It's true that, when it comes to carpeting, we tend to stick with neutral shades of beige, charcoal, cream, chocolate and straw, and in this case it's probably a good thing. Laying carpet is an expensive procedure and we need our flooring to act as a neutral third party — 'grounding' our interior, ready for the colour to be laid on top. My suggestion here is to just ensure that you keep your flooring a darker tone than your wall colour — that is, if you're going for beige, keep the walls white; if it's charcoal, keep the walls to a pale tone (of almost anything). This will maintain the sense of balance and provide the foundation for your room. If you choose a pale shade for the floor and a dominant shade for the wall you'll feel as if you are floating! Never paint the ceiling and cover the floor in the same colour (particularly if it's a darker tone); you'll be sure to feel boxed in. Remember also, that if you are decorating a small room, pale carpeting will make the room appear larger; dark carpet will make a large room appear smaller.

FLOORBOARDS

Floorboards are the closest we'll get in our homes to the feeling of being connected with nature. No doubt it has something to do with the fact that they are made from wood, and are varnished in tones that mimic the colour of the bare earth. Every time our feet touch the floorboards we are reconnected with the earth on a subconscious level. Different types of wood take on a different finish once they are varnished, so be sure to know which wood you are living with. Coat a sample area with a clear varnish first to be sure that you are happy with the colour. If you aren't satisfied, choose a tinted varnish to alter the tone. Select ebony and dark chocolate if you are after a solid base, but only go for these tones if your room is large enough to cope with their intensity. Warm tones, they imbue the boards with an orange tinge and mimic the desert earth; they are perfect if you want to create a sense of cosiness and warmth in your space. However, if your room has loads of direct sunlight this colour scheme could create an overheated effect; in this situation stick to more neutral shades. Colour washes and lime washes lighten the wood, giving it a 'washed-out' feel, perfect if you want to retain the essence and the texture of the wood but need a paler tone to suit your interior.

> '[DESIGN IS] A PLAN FOR ARRANGING ELEMENTS IN SUCH A WAY AS TO BEST ACCOMPLISH A PARTICULAR PURPOSE.'
> *CHARLES EAMES*

Using paint gives you the option to completely change the colour of the floor; I'd stay with fairly neutral tones in this case. Pure white will open up a small room, giving it the feeling of endless space. Beware though: a white floor can get very scuffed and dirty and will require daily mopping. Grey — pale if you're after a Nordic feel, charcoal for a more dramatic effect — is easier to maintain. Pale but muted green creates a laidback country feel. Black is slick and sophisticated, perfect for a classic city apartment, and works well coupled with white walls. If you are painting the floor, you will need to use a high-gloss, enamel paint to ensure that it stands up to the test of constant shoe abuse.

FLOOR TILES

An ideal choice, particularly if you are living in a warm climate, floor tiling is easy to live with and, even more importantly, effortless to keep clean. The breadth of colour choices available also makes it an interesting option. Again, here you can afford to have some fun; however, as you have probably already guessed, small spaces are the best places to employ wild colour — kitchens, bathrooms, laundry areas, around fireplaces. Choose anything from small mosaic tiles to larger tiles that form out-of-the ordinary patterning. Larger spaces call for a larger tile and more neutral colour choices. Terrazzo and concrete tiling add texture. Terracotta tiling is the most 'earthy' material that you can use — terracottas range from intense orange, which originate in Italy and Mexico, through to the pale sand tones found in many Moroccan tiles. My favourite, though, are the pale pink/orange-tinged tiles from Portugal.

A BOOK, MAGAZINES, POSTCARDS, EVEN CATALOGUES: PRINTED MEDIA ARE AN EASILY ACCESSIBLE SOURCE OF COLOUR INSPIRATION. TEAR OUT YOUR FAVOURITE COLOUR COMBINATIONS AND PASTE INTO A SCRAPBOOK AS A REFERENCE.

[conjure colour revelations
GRAPHICS]

Magazines — local or international; fashion or interior — are the best place to get access to various creative ideas without having to travel too far and without having to spend too much cash. Tear out the pictures that speak to you most compellingly and compile them into a scrapbook or inspiration folder — soon enough you will have built up a useful colour profile that defines the palette you love. Much to my husband's dismay, magazines are a stalwart that I rely on to conjure colour revelations, so much so that they have become a general part of my interior landscape (read: they're constantly strewn across and shoved into every available space). I try not to limit myself to the photographs though. Just as exciting are the graphics and the colours that the magazine designers use to embellish and highlight the words that accompany the pictures. After spending a few years working on various types of magazines I know how much effort these professionals put into creating colour schemes that are relevant both to the photographs within the magazine and to our contemporary view of colour balance and harmony. Graphic designers know colour intimately — they work with it every day and rely on it to illustrate their stories. Each magazine has a different graphic approach, as they cater to different subjects and a different audience. Although it makes sense here, since we are talking interiors, that interiors magazines would be the first port of call, don't neglect the others on offer.

Illustrated books form another enduring source of colour inspiration. Naturally, interiors books provide the most literal interpretation of the use of colour; however, you should think outside the square. Any book will work. A book on nature, on animals or perhaps on gardening will display endless shades and combinations of colours.

furniture

Your furniture is the layer of colour that you interact with the most. You sit, lounge and sleep on it — so make sure you feel comfortable.

GROUND YOUR SPACE

Now, onto the second layer of colour, which comprises the elements that ground the space: generally the larger items of furniture such as rugs, sofas, dining and coffee tables and, of course, the beds for the bedrooms. Because of their sheer scale it's impossible for the eye to avoid these pieces. Once again, you will need to start by assessing the space for which your colours are intended, and by thinking how the colours will be used to create balance. But which item comes first? Which is the piece that dictates the palette for all the other pieces? I would say it doesn't really matter, as long as you are happy that the first permanent piece of furniture you move into your room will be the guide to the colour scheme for the rest of your interior. This weighty decision is made easier if you have a broad vision for the space before you re-cover pieces, or buy them from scratch. For example, if you decide you will have a wooden dining setting and coffee tables in the room, you should have a clear idea of the tone of the wood before deciding on the colour of the sofa covering, to ensure that they blend. Make sure that timbers match to some degree, or at least come in complementary tones. That doesn't mean that you can't mix light and dark woods together — just be sure that they blend. A cherry wood, for example, mixed in with a blond wood, put together with a teak, does not make for a harmonious space; keep it simple. Use furniture in light tones if you are furnishing small rooms, saving the deep, dark timbers for your larger spaces. Offset the timber of your tables with a paint colour for your sideboard and dining chairs. It doesn't have to be a bright — simple black or white does the trick. This will prevent a glut of wood taking over the landscape of your room.

A DEEPER FURNITURE COLOUR PALETTE WORKS WELL ON A WHITE CANVAS. HERE THE DEPTH OF COLOUR IN THE SOFA AND COFFEE TABLE BALANCE THE NATURAL BRICK FIREPLACE.

THE DARK WOOD DINING TABLE AND CHAIRS PROVIDE A SOLID FOUNDATION FOR A FOLLY

When it comes to your sofa, the world is your oyster! My cherished fourteen-year-old sofa has seen many incarnations, depending on my stage in life, originating in cream (before children!); morphing into a bright cobalt blue; then moving to a Moroccan stripe in red, mauve and cream; and finally emerging a rich chocolate brown. Each phase has had its benefits, but from a decorating perspective, the solid neutrals are easiest to pair with detail colour. By keeping your sofa neutral — and by neutral I mean anything from cream to chocolate to deep midnight blue — you are providing a solid base that allows you to decorate and redecorate with creativity and flexibility, and which also allows you to change your mind without having to go to terrible expense. Having said that, don't let this advice hold you back if you are partial to bright colour and even pattern. There's nothing like a hot pink sofa or a Designers Guild style floral or stripe to remind you that you

are truly alive. If you do choose this option, keep the rest of your furnishings fairly simple to balance out the intensity. I actually think that if you want to use bold colour or patterning with a solid piece of furniture it is best to do so with a lounge chair rather than a sofa. This could be an old-style comfy chair, a designer classic or a slick-lined contemporary style — it doesn't matter. The benefit is that you get the opportunity to play around with some funky colours and designs without those designs taking over your whole room. Keep it interesting by mixing styles. A modern, clean-edged chair covered in a bold geometric floral in bright colours does a lot to add interest to an essentially neutral space.

The bedroom, that most private of places, is a room where you can unleash your colour passion. The bed is the major player here, so dress it with comfort and decadence in mind. Remember, not everything has to match. Mix colours for your top and bottom sheet and perhaps choose a pattern combining the two colours for your duvet or bedspread. Reintroduce a solid colour for a throw rug that sits at the end of the bed. Cushions in highlight colours can sit atop the pillows. An all-white bed with a highlight colour used only for the throw rug and the cushions will create an open, airy space and make you feel as though you are resting on clouds. Sandy tones will warm up the space a little. Refer back to Chapter 2 when making your colour choices, as colour affects us intensely when we are resting.

fabric

The textiles that you employ tell the story of your interior, more so than any other element.

CHOOSING FABRIC

It's at about this stage, when fabric comes into play, that things really start to get interesting — or tricky, depending on your perspective. It is fabric that facilitates our creative fancy, more so than any other medium, and so it's an aspect of decorating that we really need to have a grip on if we are to make our home a true reflection of ourselves. This isn't easy: step into almost any fabric store and you will see thousands upon thousands of fabrics; you'll probably feel like a kid in a candy store — overwhelmed by choice and desire! Even the die-hard decorators among us can feel daunted. My reaction is generally one of freneticism. I want everything! Before I arrived at the store I wouldn't even have considered the idea of chinoiserie in shades of pink and mint green in lush satin fabrics (I'm more of a deep brown and rusty red girl) — but once inside

I'm at the mercy of the endless possibilities. Avoiding this reaction does take a certain amount of discipline. Here are a few pointers that will keep you on the right track both while you are selecting your fabrics and once you have brought them home.

SET PARAMETERS

Have an idea of what you want before you head out to the fabric houses. (That is, go through Chapters 1 and 2 of this book before you get to this point.) Narrow your options. Think, at least, of the base colour that you would like to use and when you arrive at the fabric houses move straight to that section.

ASK THE PROFESSIONALS

Ask the shop assistants for advice. Give them an idea of what you are looking for and they will steer you in the right direction. No doubt they will pull out certain fabrics that fit your description. This way, you avoid having to go through the whole plethora of fabrics — and you gain the benefit of their knowledge.

SWATCHES OF FABRIC, IN A MYRIAD OF COLOURS, ARE AS EXCITING A PROSPECT FOR AN INTERIORS ENTHUSIAST AS CANDY IS TO A CHILD. AH, THE POSSIBILITIES!

IDENTIFY YOUR COLOUR SYSTEM

Choose fabrics in two stages — first select the base fabric and then pick the secondary fabric or fabrics. I prefer to get my base colour down pat before I get into further detail with fabric choice; however, working backwards is an option, even though it can be more difficult to match colours this way. Most rooms can generally cope with a two-colour system: the main colour and then an accent or contrasting colour. I like to push the envelope and go for a three-colour system, as adding layers provides visual interest — although I would get the first two colours right before trying for the third. Avoid more than three colours, as you'll end up with a messy palette, unless you are a very proficient decorator.

RESEARCH

Never buy on the first shopping date. Take your time, gather your swatches, create a mood board, arrange and then rearrange the colour combinations. Visit a few different stores and slowly you'll start to see some kind of palette emerging. Live with the palette for a while. Move it around different parts of the room to see how it responds to different light sources. Layer your colours to see how different shades and patterns react to each other. Once you feel good about your choices, invest in a metre (about three feet) of each of the fabrics and drape them on the furniture you intend to cover. Again, live with it; see how each fabric reacts to different light. Once you feel confident about your choices — buy!

BALANCE THE EFFECT

When it comes to colour, it's all about balance. Once you have chosen your colour scheme, ensure that those colours are balanced throughout the room. Having all of your pinks down one end of the room, and all of your mauves down the other, will leave the space looking lopsided. Blend each colour throughout the space. It doesn't have to be a completely even dispersion; a cushion here or a throw there could be enough. Use your eye to gauge the results, then assess how you feel in the space. If you gain an impression of balance, then you've done your job.

BREAK UP BLOCKS OF COLOUR

Once your main pieces are covered, look at how you can break up those large blocks of colour with smaller blocks. For example, an oversized sofa covered in a block fabric could benefit from a string of cushions in a contrasting colour or a pattern. If your windows are covered with patterned curtains, place a solid colour in front of them — say, a sofa or armchair. If the rug on the floor is intricately patterned, a block colour for the sofa or the coffee table is a good option.

WRITE YOURSELF A CHECKLIST OF ALL THE THINGS THAT YOU NEED YOUR FABRIC TO DO FOR YOUR SPACE, BEFORE YOU HEAD OUT SHOPPING. THEN RUN THROUGH YOUR LIST AS YOU'RE PERUSING THE OPTIONS. IF THE FABRIC DOESN'T GET A TICK IN EVERY BOX, THEN IT'S NOT RIGHT.

PATTERN

Colour and pattern go hand in hand in an interior, working together to create depth and meaning in what could otherwise be a fairly bland environment. How you approach pattern, and how that pattern relates to your colour choices, will define the type of interior you create. I think that it's fairly accurate to say that block patterns in geometric shapes work to create a bold, contemporary environment. The famous Marimekko fabric house that combines black and white with bold colour and simplicity of shape, saves even the most modern interiors from being cold and stark. The clean lines of Florence Broadhurst fabrics and wallpapers — although slightly more intricate in design — evoke a sense of modernity through the patterning, even though the designs are now decades old. Combine these bold shapes with soft colour, however, and the look moves from highly contemporary to Nordic in feel — simply through a shift in the colour scheme.

Intricate patterning creates a different feel, which is also affected by your colour choices. Complex patterns in stately tones of burgundy and gold create a sense of grandeur in a room — the type of feel that you'll find in classic old homes. Combine the same patterning with a palette of pale pinks and greens and you end up with a more feminine space. Go for bright cobalt blue or even black and white, and you have a classic space with a contemporary twist.

Florals work in a similar way. The bold, sweeping florals in tones of bright pink and orange that you'll find in Designers Guild fabrics add energy and excitement to a space. The same pattern in muted earthy tones creates a rustic feel. Small floral patterns in pretty colours, like the Shabby Chic range of fabrics, hark back to times past. Combine those same fabrics with simple block colours for your sofa, and you'll add a modern twist. If you prefer a contemporary feel but would like to infuse florals into your space, choose fresh, brightly coloured florals like those in the Cath Kidston range of fabrics.

Combining patterns can be an art form; but it is not completely out of reach of the home decorator, and I recommend working in stages to avoid becoming overwhelmed. Start out with your base, block colour, as always. Let's say for the sake of argument that it's chocolate brown. Next, go for a stripe; I love the ticking varieties that combine the chocolate brown with a second colour — this could be pink (with perhaps a hint of cream or white to allow the pattern to breathe). Then move into your block florals — chocolate, pink, perhaps more cream or white; this is where your third colour can come into play. Let's say orange! Once your block florals are in place, choose your intricate florals, which could be a sample of the abovementioned colour scheme. Always vary the size of the furniture items to be covered, to avoid all the patterns competing for the same amount of attention.

TEXTURE

Not all fabrics are created equal, and of course, besides their colour differences, there are textural differences — each working to evoke a certain mood in your home. For you to truly relax in your home and be at one with your space, the textures have to work to lull you into a state of relaxation and comfort. Just as you may consider slinky satin textures relaxing, the next person may prefer the crispness of linen, so it is a very personal response. Like all the other elements of design, texture has an impact on your colour choices. Deep, plush velvets will enrich any colour, even brights. Run your hand across the velvet and notice how the colour graduates in tone, from light to dark. Because of its richness, velvet also absorbs light, so it is perfect if you want to minimize glare. Satins and silks reflect light and bounce colour around a room and are an ideal option if you want to increase the amount of light in a space. Linens embody a certain raw, earthy quality; as the weave is generally loose, they will often absorb colour, resulting in a soft, muted feel, even when used with bright fabrics.

Texture can be applied to a room not only through fabrics but also through paint and wallpaper. Roughly textured sand or 'suede' paints and lime washes add varying tones of the same colour to the wall to which they are applied, creating a quality of richness — the walls will feel almost alive beneath your hand. The effect works particularly well with deep colours of purple and blue. Metallic paints are to walls what satins are to fabrics, throwing light around the room, making your space feel electric and playful. Metallic shades of pink, white and blue are good choices. Flocked wallpapers, which combine a smooth base colour with a raised textured pattern, add depth to colours and interest to a space.

Mood boards and wonder walls

A mood board is a great way to capture a sense of the effect you are trying to achieve. It is a bit like a taste test: you can try, and see what you do and don't like, before you buy. Mood boards mean different things to different people. I use them to evoke a sense of the things that I love, in two ways.

For me, photographs of my travels represent a mood board. I don't know about you, but when I travel, I'm not a snap happy kind of girl, photographing everything that comes into sight. Instead, I like to think I'm a little more discerning, taking photographs of the things that really appeal to me — whether that be a market full of brightly coloured fruit, a woman's traditional dress, a landscape, children playing in the street or even the colour of a bicycle. When you photograph this way your shots begin to form a clear picture of the things you are drawn to. You'll begin to notice a thread of colour emerging, or favourite patterns — perhaps intricately carved woodwork or detailed artwork. Go back through your pictures and I'm sure they'll tell the story of your loves.

The other way to capture an overall sense of your personal aesthetic is through a wonder wall. When I was a child, I would pin up pictures of those things I loved all over my bedroom wall, lie in bed and dream about the possibilities of my life. Even now that I'm older I still have a wonder wall — although these days it's a small section of wall above the computer in my office. Here I pin up everything from fabric swatches, through to postcards, photographs and pictures torn from magazines — anything that moves me. It's certainly a great starting point. Perhaps you're more of a workbook person — filing and pasting all of your swatches of fabric and other colour cues into a pint-sized, easily transportable filing system. It doesn't really matter how you tap into your inspiration; these are but a few of the possibilities. Just do what works for you.

inspiration beyond the domestic
[PUBLIC SPACES]

Of course, your most obvious port of call when looking for colour inspiration for your interior is — other interiors. What better way to see interior design ideas come to life? After all, the ways in which people create an interior, the inspiration that they draw on and the life experiences that are personified through their homes form the focus of this book. But when we're talking interiors, why stop at the home? Design and decorating and thus colour have permeated so many other aspects of contemporary living that there is a myriad of ideas available for you to draw on. The restaurant, for example, is often no longer just a place to enjoy a meal; these days, it's about serving good food in a well-thought-out, stimulating environment. As a result, in many cases what was once your visually unstimulating local restaurant has now become a breeding ground for contemporary design and a source of inspiration for you to draw on; bars and nightclubs the same.

Shop interiors are loaded with ideas. Naturally, interiors stores are my favourite. There's so much 'stuff' from which to extract inspiration: not just the colours and patterns used in the framework of the room but also the bits and bobs that are on sale — they are a great way to see how colour combinations work together. A try before you buy kind of thing!

Don't forget the 'boutique' hotel. In contrast to the bland chain hotels, boutique hotels are mostly privately owned, and their interiors often reflect the owner's aesthetic rather than being designed to appeal to the general population. If you're looking to be inspired in a different way, book a weekend away and explore the creativity employed in these wonderful places — and remember to take a camera to record the details.

display

I'm not a big one for creating a specific look – Moroccan, say, or African – unless of course that look evolves organically from the nature of the pieces you choose to display together.

Often, it's the pieces that we display in our homes that give our living spaces a certain flavour. I like to think about the detail that you apply to your home as the final layer of colour. The icing on the cake perhaps! It's the stuff that really rounds out an interior, giving your space a sense of individuality and personality. What you choose to display tells the most about who you are, where you've been, and where you're going. Sometimes the only colour in a room is infused through the detail; or perhaps the colour in the detail serves to add weight to your general colour scheme.

COLLECTIONS

What you collect reads like a window into your soul. It tells a lot about who you are and what interests you and lends a fascinating extra dimension to your colour scheme. Grouping collections into colour themes provides each vignette with depth. If your pieces are multicoloured, then group them with the base colour. A mantelpiece filled with coloured glass ornaments in variations of the same tone looks stylish. A collection of woven baskets in muted earth tones can be stacked in a quiet corner to liven up the space. Books on the bookshelf are more pleasing to the eye when they are arranged in groups of the same colour. Even a simple gesture, such as a group of the same coloured candles on the side of the bath, creates visual interest.

CUSHIONS AND THROWS

Instead of matching your scatter cushions and throw rugs with the general theme of your upholstered fabrics, why not source them independently and use them as accents for your base colour scheme? There's nothing more interesting than a sofa filled with cushions that each tell a tale. On my day bed, I've mixed a patterned kilim cushion from Turkey and a chenille cushion found at a homewares store with a hand-me-down from my mother. All share the same colour scheme, or variations of, but each tells a different story and means something to me in a very different way. The result is a mix of colour, pattern and interest.

DON'T IGNORE COLOUR WHEN DISPLAYING YOUR MANY TREASURES. THESE ITEMS, THE FINAL LAYER, CAN BRING THE WHOLE COLOUR PALETTE TOGETHER.

[SENSEOFSTYLECOLOUR] TELLS THE STORY, AND ANY OTHER COLOUR WOULD DETRACT FROM THE INTENSITY.

SOMETIMES THE COLOURS OF A SINGLE PAINTING ARE ALL THAT A SPACE REQUIRES. THE PAINTING ITSELF

ARTWORK

Even the blandest interior is brought to life when artwork graces the walls. Choosing art is a personal adventure, because you are buying not only the form and colour of the piece, but also the story of the artist who has created it. Fuse that with your own personal story and you have a very colourful and significant decorating tool. The artwork that you choose doesn't have to fit into the general decorating landscape. It can be the one piece that stands alone, jolting the senses, a talking piece. However, I do feel that if you are searching for a harmonious interior, your art should incorporate tones of the colours that you have used in decorating. The general lounge room interior in my home is brown and orange, with a touch of cream, and my contrast piece is a bright green chair. I have mimicked the green of the chair with a couple of paintings that combine touches of

green, which I have hung on an adjacent wall at the other end of the room. Artwork is a colour tool that helps to balance out a space. Just as you may group colourful collections together on a table, think about grouping similarly coloured paintings on the same wall.

FLOWERS

Sometimes, colour can be but a token gesture in a room, rather than the focus, and in this way flowers can do the trick. An all-neutral interior punctuated by an oversized vase of bright pink peonies is a significant colour burst in an otherwise colourless space. If you like the idea of a harmonious two-colour interior but would like occasional oomph, use flowers as the third colour when you feel like it. If you have a highly colourful interior, choose a bunch of the same coloured flowers rather than a mix to add weight to your colour scheme. And sometimes a single flower is all that's required.

this goes with that

Trying to connect with your senses but having trouble visualizing your ideal colour combinations? Well, this is for those of you in need of a more formulaic approach to colour.

Okay, so I've succumbed and this section is for those of you who have read through the book; spent hours gazing across landscapes filled with flowers; reflected on your likes and dislikes; put together walls of wonder; gone shopping for inspiration; eaten countless chocolate bars — but still can't discern what goes with what! So, just for you, here is a short lesson on the colour wheel.

There are three primary colours: red, blue and yellow. By mixing these colours in equal quantities you create the secondary family of colours:

red + blue = purple

blue + yellow = green

yellow + red = orange

By varying the quantity of each colour, you get what's called tertiary colours or tones of the secondary colour. Colours that sit next to each other on the colour wheel are referred to as harmonious colours — those that are opposite each other are contrasting colours. Generally, an interior will feature two harmonious colours and a contrasting colour for interest. If you are opting for a two-colour system, choose your base colour and add a contrasting colour to that.

Of course, there are tints of colours — that is where you add a little black or white to the mix — and tones of the same colour. The choices are endless and the number of colours that can be created is overwhelming; however, if you are really stuck and can't rely on your own senses to lead you to your personal palette, following the colour wheel system is a failsafe method until you have built up your confidence. Perhaps you can use this method to get your base colour scheme organized, and then play around with the detail using your own instincts. Whatever you do though, don't miss out on the opportunity to really connect with yourself and your sense of style by letting your intuition guide you to an interior that truly reflects who you are. It may be tricky and time consuming, but I promise that it will lead you to a home that you love living in — a home that you feel at one with. And that's what home should be.

USE TACTILE OBJECTS TO CREATE YOUR COLOUR WHEEL. BALLS OF WOOL CAN BE HELD IN THE HAND, TOUCHED AND PLAYED WITH TO HELP YOU VISUALIZE WHICH COLOURS GO WITH WHAT.

colour connection

SO, HERE WE ARE AT THE CONCLUSION
OF OUR COLOUR JOURNEY. HOPEFULLY, IF YOU'VE ARRIVED AT THIS POINT
YOU'VE FOLLOWED MY ADVICE AND TAKEN THE TIME
TO JUST SIT FOR A WHILE AND LOOK AROUND YOU.

INFUSE COLOUR INTO YOUR HOME THROUGH THE THINGS YOU LOVE — WHETHER THEY BE LARGE OR SMALL, HUMBLE OR HIGH DESIGN. THEN SIT DOWN, HAVE A CUP OF TEA, AND ENJOY WATCHING YOUR COLOUR PALETTE UNFOLD BEFORE YOU.

In simply doing that you have taken the first step towards connecting with colour. Although there is a certain amount of seriousness involved in unearthing your sense of style, please don't be too earnest about the process! Always keep in mind that colour is supposed to be fun — and the process of infusing colour into your home should inspire the same kind of excitement that a child feels at the onset of colouring-in a drawing. Just as a child uses their intuition to guide them through their colour choices, you can use yours to help guide you through your decorating choices and set you on the path to creating an individual space, unique to your life and experiences.

If you have reached the point of making confident colour choices, then I think that it's safe to say you're on the road to developing your own sense of style. So with that I'll say good luck, have fun, and enjoy the wonderful gift that is colour.

index

Published by Murdoch Books Pty Limited

Murdoch Books Pty Limited Australia

Pier 8/9, 23 Hickson Road, Millers Point NSW 2000

Phone: + 61 (0) 2 8220 2000 Fax: + 61 (0) 2 8220 2558

Website: www.murdochbooks.com.au

Murdoch Books UK Limited

Erico House, 6th Floor North,

93–99 Upper Richmond Road, Putney, London SW15 2TG

Phone: + 44 (0) 20 8785 5995 Fax: + 44 (0) 20 8785 5985

Chief Executive: Juliet Rogers
Publishing Director: Kay Scarlett

Design Manager: Vivien Valk
Editor: Diana Hill
Concept and design: Lauren Camilleri
Production: Maiya Levitch

National Library of Australia
Cataloguing-in-Publication Data:
Fricke, Shannon.
Sense of style: Colour
Includes index. ISBN 978 1 74045 805 4.
ISBN 1 74045 805 2. 1. Color in interior
decoration. 2. House furnishings. I. Title. 747.94

Printed by 1010 International Limited.
Printed in China